ALL BEADED UP

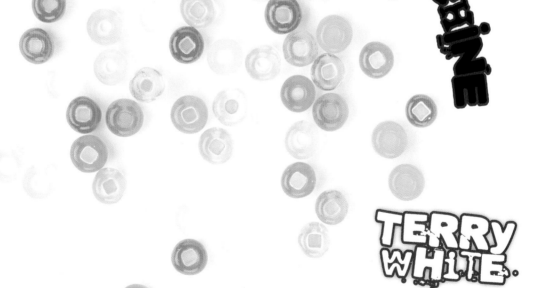

BY MACHINE

TERRY WHITE

American Quilter's Society

P. O. Box 3290 • Paducah, KY 42002-3290
www.AmericanQuilter.com

Located in Paducah, Kentucky, the American Quilter's Society (AQS) is dedicated to promoting the accomplishments of today's quilters. Through its publications and events, AQS strives to honor today's quiltmakers and their work and to inspire future creativity and innovation in quiltmaking.

EXECUTIVE EDITOR: ANDI MILAM REYNOLDS
SENIOR EDITOR: LINDA BAXTER LASCO
GRAPHIC DESIGN: ELAINE WILSON
COVER DESIGN: MICHAEL BUCKINGHAM
QUILT AND STEP-BY-STEP TECHNIQUE PHOTOGRAPHY: CHARLES R. LYNCH
ADDITIONAL PHOTOGRAPHY: TERRY WHITE

Additional copies of this book may be ordered from the American Quilter's Society, PO Box 3290, Paducah, KY 42002-3290, or online at www.AmericanQuilter.com.

Text © 2008, Author, Terry White
Artwork © 2008, American Quilter's Society

Library of Congress Cataloging-in-Publication Data

White, Terry.
  All beaded up by machine / by Terry White.
      p. cm.
  ISBN 978-1-57432-969-8
  1. Beadwork. 2. Machine sewing. I. Title.

TT860.W588 2008
746.5--dc22

                                        2008042208

American Quilter's Society
P. O. Box 3290 • Paducah, KY 42002-3290
www.AmericanQuilter.com

Proudly printed and bound in the United States of America

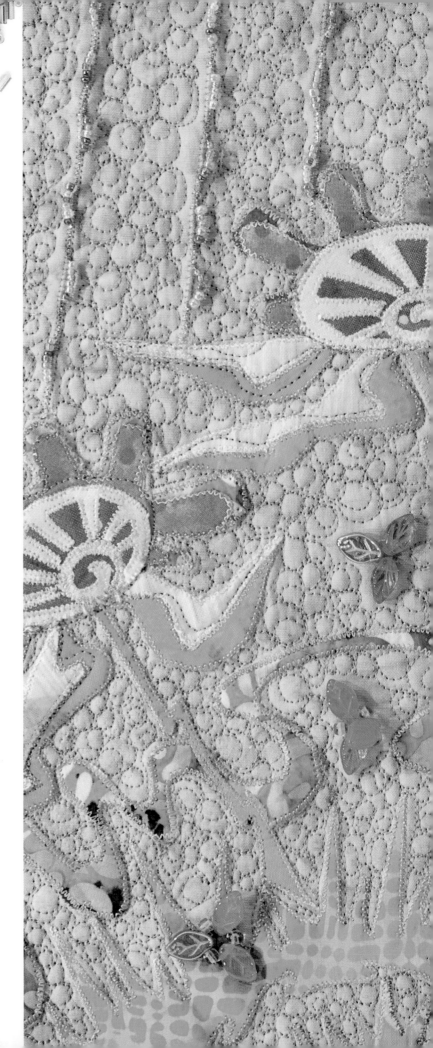

Dedication

In loving memory of my sister, Kat, and my dad, Tony. They would have loved this.

And to my mom, Trish, artist and designer, who made sure we had all the arts and crafts supplies. We are a creative family because of her. I love you, Mom.

Acknowledgments

Thank you Scot, my dear husband, for your forever love and your constancy in helping me to get my work done. Thank you Liz, Robby, Russell, and Krista, our grown-up kids, for your humor, excitement, and drama that I need to stay involved with life while I'm trying to get my work done. Thank you my dear sister Mary Ann, creative brother Wally, and smart sister-in-law Mary, for your constant humor and appreciation for this kooky journey we are on. Thank you my Bob and Jean for your constant love and support.

Thank you, my girlfriends Lisa, Sue, Betty, Deb, Sanna, Nicole, and Sharon. You keep my nose to the grindstone and let it up when it is getting rubbed raw. You inspire me to do better and keep me laughing at myself. I am lost without my girls!

With this, my second book, I must express my appreciation for the incredible support, creativity, and overall expertise of the great people at American Quilter's Society Publishing.

Thank you, Linda Baxter Lasco, my editor, for your help, understanding, humor, and editing work.

Thank you, Elaine Wilson, my book designer! You are a wonderful artist and designer. You made this book beautiful and happy!

Thank you, John Carr and Jeanne Delpit of Bernina for getting an Artista 730 into my hands. Even though I can stitch my techniques on a variety of machines, this one does it with great craftsmanship and beauty. It is a peach of a machine!

Thank you, my friend Nancy Jewell of Coats & Clark for the beautiful array of Star multicolor cottons and metallic threads. The color mixes of the variegated threads are quite delicious and several spools were the color inspiration for projects. The metallic threads perform beautifully for thread painting and decorative sewing machine stitches.

Thank you, Jane Garrison of YLI for the luscious gimp and threads used in the projects.

Thank you, Clare Rowley of Creative Feet for the great feet, information, and inspiration for the future.

Thank you, thank you, thank you all!
Terry

Contents

Introduction

Beading has always been an integral part of my needlework. I've hand stitched beads onto needlepoint, embroidery, appliqué, and pieced work and I've quilted with beads. So, just as I now embroider, quilt, piece, appliqué, and embellish with the use of my sewing machine, I also bead by machine.

I developed these techniques when I could no longer bead by hand. My hands wouldn't do it anymore. The techniques presented here do not intend to replace hand beading, they are simply an alternative technique.

Developing the variations on the basic technique has been an interesting experimental time. What can be done with this kind of bead? How can different sizes be mixed? What will this fabric or yarn mixed with the beads look like? How can I achieve a certain look, texture, or detail with the addition of beads?

The techniques presented are my experiments. The projects provide an opportunity to put these techniques into practice. I have included a variety of projects with varied color schemes and design ideas to show the variety of work that can be achieved with these techniques. I will show you many ways that different types of beads and fibers can be used together and I'll suggest ways to use colors.

There are some additional techniques included that are not done by machine. I call one of these techniques "bead clusters." It employs minimal hand stitching and I love it because it's pretty. I also occasionally will hand stitch a single bead or button when it is called for. Don't be surprised.

I hope this book will be an inspiration and also a point of departure for you to discover your own way to use beads in your needlework journey.

So, let's bead!

Terry White
2008

Begin at the Beginning

The essential technique put forth in this book is simply this—string beads on a thread and then couch (stitch over) the thread between the beads to secure them to the fabric. This came to me after pondering the problem of machine beading for a month back in January of 2002.

While developing the technique, I found that there was no tool that would effectively push the beads away from the machine foot so the couching stitches could be done. So my husband and I developed "The Beadle" (see the Resources, page 94). To me, it is more efficient than a bent wire, which is what I used at first. Since that time, I have worked and played with variations on the machine beading theme. I produced a machine beading video in 2004 and since then have expanded and improved the technique.

Four basic machine-beading techniques:

① Couch the bead string with a decorative machine stitch.

② Bar-tack yarn with bead string wrap.

③ Couch the bead string loosely, being sure not to catch the bead string, then draw it taut to bring the beads in place.

④ Free-motion beading.

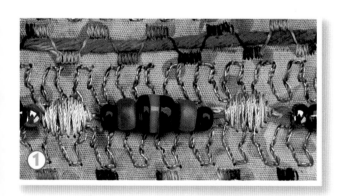

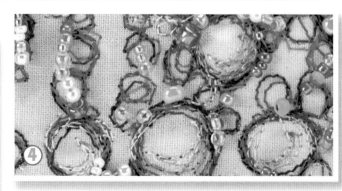

Working with these four techniques suggested even more variations to me. For example, when I was stopped by wanting to use a certain yarn with a group of beads and the bead holes were too small for the yarn, I simply stitched down the yarn first so the bead string accented the yarn as I machine beaded over it (a).

The bar-tack lent itself to all kinds of variations.

A woman at the American Quilter's Society Quilt Show & Contest in Paducah suggested a variation in method to me. She suggested using the ankle of the presser foot with no foot attached. I need to find that lady and thank her with all my heart and tell everyone her name! This idea is so good. Many machines don't have the feet I suggest using, so this method is good for them and has added techniques to this needle art form, including quilting a beaded surface (b).

I ultimately developed three more techniques and there are instructions for all seven in the Step-by-Step Basic Techniques section (pages 28–39). The projects in this book use these techniques with variations of bead groupings and novelty threads along with piecing, appliqué, and thread painting.

I am specific about the materials used for each project so that you, the stitcher, can see how the different threads, yarns, fabrics, and beads work together. The variety of combinations is endless.

It would be practically impossible to find the exact combination of beads and threads that I used. Use the supply lists as a guide to find comparable materials and feel free to make your own choices. The projects are vehicles, inspiration, and suggestions as to how to apply the techniques. I want you to have as much fun making them as I did.

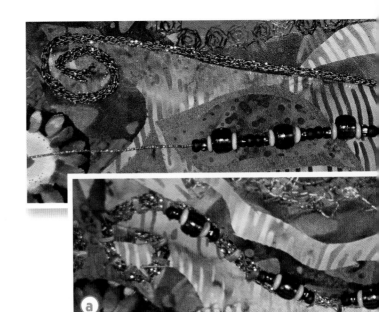

There is a learning curve to these techniques. I suggest practicing before working on a project. When I have been away from beading for a while, I always do a little practicing to get in the groove again before working on a project.

Tools, Toys, and Technical Info

Years ago, when I managed a fabric store, somebody gave me a pin that declared, "My toys! Where are my toys? I can't do this job without my toys!" We don't just need our toys, we love them!

The Beadle

Scot and I developed this little tool to aid in the work of beading by machine. The wire holds the beads back from the needle so the needle doesn't hit a bead. The wire is soft enough that it will bend before breaking a needle. The presser foot can ride over the wire and it doesn't impede the stitching. The handle has a nice feel to it, making it easy to use . . . and it looks like a beetle.

The decorative stitch technique is the one for which I invented the Beadle tool, but it comes in handy on several of the techniques.

Bead Spinner

A bead spinner allows you to string beads—lots of beads—in a short time. I found this little tool in a great bead shop and I couldn't believe how fast it works. It was made for seed beads but I have used it with bead mixes including E-beads, square beads, rocks, etc. There is a little learning curve with it—like riding a bike—but once you've got it, you've got it.

A special wire needle is threaded and then inserted into the bowl of the spinner. As the bowl spins, the beads are fed onto this needle and then strung along the bead string. The bead string is then cut from the wire needle and threaded onto a hand needle to be secured to the fabric.

The bead spinner is used for random bead mixes or when the order of the beads is not important to the project.

Bead Organization

The more beads you have, the bigger the issue of organization becomes. This corner of my studio is home to my beads.

I have a variety of storage items, including an antique chest for watch crystals, a wooden unit made by a craftsman (purchased years ago at an AQS quilt show), a hardware unit with little drawers, and plastic shoe boxes.

There are many options for storing and organizing beads. Shop craft, hardware, container, and discount stores for storage options. It is fun to repurpose items found in flea markets and yard sales, too. The important thing is that the beads are ordered in such a way as to make them accessible to you and the way that you work.

I organize my beads first by color and then by type, because color is always my first consideration when selecting beads for a project.

My father-in-law, Bob, gave me this Chinese apothecary chest for my birthday. He thought it would be great for my buttons and beads. It is!

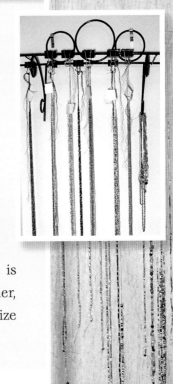

Here are bead strings ready to use. After stringing them with the bead spinner, I knot them to a clip and hang them from this flea market find—a shelf rack with the glass shelf missing.

This piece of drapery linen hanging from a curtain rod is where I hang the bead strings that are strung without the spinner, either because I wanted a formal arrangement or because the size or irregular shape of the beads wouldn't work in the spinner.

It is great to have a lot of bead strings ready before beginning a project, and these hanging options keep the beads in sight and tangle free.

Hoop

Scot found this Morgan hoop at a 2006 quilt show and it is a peach. It is the best hoop I have found for holding the fabric taut with no slipping. This is important when thread painting with beads. When I have to move the hoop from one area to another, I wrap the hoop with some fabric to protect the beads or fasten the fabric to just one of the rings with binder clips.

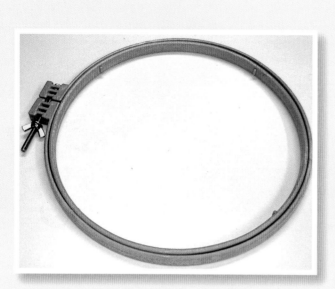

Hand Needles

As a former hand quilter with plenty of needles, I found that my size 10 or 12 hand quilting needles are small enough to go through seed beads. The hand needle is only used to string the beads and to anchor the bead string to your project with a few stitches.

Sewing Machine

You do not need a fancy machine with all kinds of bells and whistles for this kind of work. Your machine should have good stitch quality. Many of the techniques can be done simply with the bar tack, zigzag stitch, and straight stitch. Utility stitches make beautiful decorative stitches when done with pretty threads and create some wonderful effects when sewn in side-by-side rows.

Machine Needles

I use embroidery machine needles because I'm embroidering over the bead strings. And I

TIPS FOR SEWING MACHINE WORK

Be sure that your sewing machine is in good working order, cleaned, and oiled (if applicable) before you start any kind of stitching.

When couching over threads, keep in mind that you are asking your top thread to do more traveling than usual. Your sewing machine doesn't know this. Loosen the top tension to give the top thread freer flow so that it can travel over the cords and bead strings.

Check the default setting on your sewing machine for any of the embroidery stitches. It should be looser than a regular sewing stitch. You want the decorative stitches to add dimension and lie nicely on the fabric without puckering it. Use 30-weight or heavier embroidery thread for fuller looking stitches.

like to use thick machine threads. Although you should choose a needle size appropriate for the heaviness of the fabric and thickness of the thread, I find that a 90/14 works for most projects. I use a 75/11 needle with thinner threads and lighterweight fabrics.

The Feet

A variety of sewing machine feet is essential for some of the techniques in this book.

An **open-toed embroidery foot** has toes that ride the feed dogs so that the embroidery stitches stitch out well. The open center gives you visibility into what is going on, which simplifies some of the techniques in this book.

A **free-motion** or **darning foot** is important for free-motion work with beads and fill techniques.

A **beading foot,** also sometimes called a **pearls and piping foot** or an **embellishment foot,** has a large channel under the center needle position. This allows a bead string to pass through without impeding the stitch formation of decorative stitches. The one on the right is made specifically for my machine. The one on the left is from Creative Feet, which makes specialty feet designed to fit all sewing machines (see Resources, page 94).

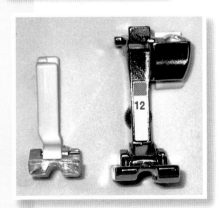

Sewing with Ankle Only

Some techniques work best using just the ankle of your presser foot. Use this option when the foot would interfere with your stitching or possibly damage the beads you've already sewn, as when you're doing free-motion beading. Without a foot, the needle can pull the fabric up along with some of the bobbin thread. This results in loose bobbin thread on the back called "flagging." Eventually, the top thread will loosen as well.

Removing the foot but leaving the ankle will help prevent flagging. Hooping the fabric and using extra stabilizer on the back of the work will also help. Use an ankle-only setup for free-motion quilting on your beaded work. If you use a Bernina® sewing machine, the ankle is not separate from the foot. I use an ankle from Creative Feet that is made for the Bernina.

Extension Table

An extension table is helpful if your machine is not set into a cabinet. It gives you a larger work space and aids in good tension and ease of stitching.

Stabilizers

Stabilizers are crucial to this work. A stabilizer adds strength and structure to the fabric on which stitching and beads are applied. It helps prevent distortion in the stitching process and keeps the beads from sagging on the finished project.

The weight of the stabilizer should be chosen according to the intended use of the project. The type and weight of the stabilizer should be included in test samples that you make before stitching on your project.

Different stabilizer types are necessary for different fabric types.

For quilter's weight cotton, the stabilizer should be nonwoven and a medium weight. The nonwoven stabilizer has no structure to compete with that of the cotton. This medium weight can be achieved by using two layers of lightweight nonwoven stabilizer. The separate layers are easier for the machine to stitch through and give the same stability that the medium weight does. Depending on the stitches used and the weight of the beads, more layers of stabilizer can be added.

I have used as many as six layers of lightweight stabilizer on some heavily beaded projects.

For clothing, a knit interfacing is a good choice. The knit will help maintain the soft drape of the fabric. For a box cover, the stabilizer should be stiffer to give good structure to the project.

For the projects shown in this book, the stabilizer should be permanent and not be cut or dissolved. The stabilizer helps to maintain the shape and structure of the project when it is finished and in use.

Glue Reinforcement

In cases where you feel extra reinforcement is required (for example, on handbags or pillows), glue a piece of fabric to the back of the work. Lightly brush fabric glue to a stabilizing fabric and apply to the back of the finished work. Lightly press with your hands. This will keep stitches and beads in place. Do this before sewing a beaded panel into the project.

Another option is to fuse a backing onto the finished work. It is the same idea as used in some looped or hooked types of needlework with the added reinforcement of rubber painted on the back. The backing prevents the threads from loosening over time.

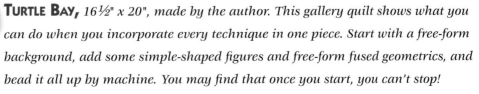

TURTLE BAY, *16½" x 20", made by the author. This gallery quilt shows what you can do when you incorporate every technique in one piece. Start with a free-form background, add some simple-shaped figures and free-form fused geometrics, and bead it all up by machine. You may find that once you start, you can't stop!*

The Bead Mix

Here are beads made from rocks, shells, pearls, clay, seeds and wood (a).

Beads are jewelry to us, embellishments, toys, shiny bright beautiful things. They can remind us of seeds, rocks, shells, candy. Beads are made of glass, wood, plastic, shells, semi-precious stones, paper, clay, etc.

The Bead Mix

There are great mixes that you can buy, and it may be a way to learn how to mix beads to get great colors. For a totally unique look, you can create your own bead mix.

The mix should be made for the purpose of the project. Choose bead sizes that fit the size of the project. The colors may blend well or be in stark contrast. In the case of high contrast, the beads become a design element and should be integrated into the design as such. Beads that blend into the surface design add a textural quality that may not be noticeable at first glance and must be studied more closely by the viewer.

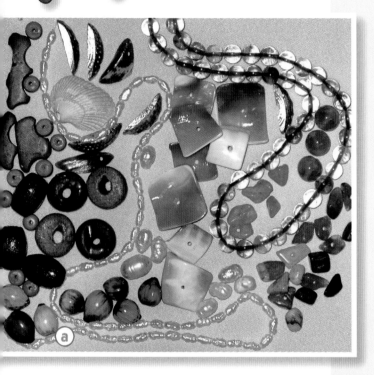

I always test my mixes by stitching them as I will on the project, using the same beads, threads, and fabrics to see how they work and look.

Random Bead Mixes

A random bead mix includes a variety of shapes, sizes, styles, and colors. Color-specific random mixes are my favorite. Sometimes I make a bead mix for a project and if there is a little left over, I dump it. I call it bead compost. Lovely things can grow from this mix (b).

The photo shows a pink and black bead mix. What are the colors between pink and black? My answer is mauve, root beer, amethyst, purple, and maroon. I added metallic beads of gold, brass, gunmetal, and copper color. The sizes range from the smallest seed beads to some 8mm pearls and E beads. When mixing beads, you can almost tell how the bead string will look. This mix will give a rich, textural look to a project.

Here are bead strings in a black to pink range (c).

Color Blends

A blend of shades of a single color can be more interesting than using a single type of bead.

This single-color bead mix shows the use of colors that blend with purple. The addition of blue, maroon, pink, copper, brown, and gold beads creates color interest in the primarily purple mix (d).

This single-color bead mix shows the use of colors that blend with green (e).

When mixing various size beads, be careful not to put a very small bead next to a bead with a large opening. The little bead might slip into the big bead. Graduate the size of beads between the big and small beads to avoid this problem.

Patterning with Beads

When creating an allover pattern for a project, making bead strings of different size beads enhances the pattern (f).

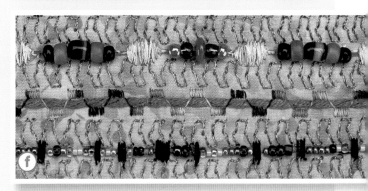

Bead Sources

I started my bead collection as a pre-teen when I was making "love bead" necklaces. I used them in needlepoint, crewel embroidery, and lace work. When I began to quilt in 1978, it wasn't long before my beads were added to wall quilts, quilted vests, handbags, quilted toys, and puppets.

I find beads everywhere! I take apart jewelry I find at yard sales and flea markets. A friend of mine once gave me a ruined beaded dress. It took several evenings sitting in front of the TV to cut the beads from that dress, but the harvest of aubergine glass beads was so worth it. Once I found a junk shop that had beads from India. I was sifting in the beads so long that the owner brought out a heavy box and sold it to me for a few dollars. When I got it home, I spent several evenings separating the red, blue, green, purple, brown, white, black, and yellow beads. There was a huge variety of glass beads.

Every quilt, craft, or sewing show that I go to, I visit and buy from all the bead vendors. I want them to stay in business! Each one is unique and has interesting things to sell.

I shop for beads in bead stores and craft shops. Once again, I want them to stay in business so I can buy beads forever.

When I need beads and I know I won't be able to find them in my corner of the world, I will order from mail order bead companies. Everyone has their favorite and mine is Fire Mountain Gems. Their catalog is free and is an incredible resource.

Learning about Beads

There are so many kinds of beads you can spend lots of time learning about them. The resources are endless.

Price Matters

The more expensive beads are usually more uniform in size and made of high quality materials. Less expensive ones are more cheaply made. The materials used may be plastic or acrylic. Choose the best beads that you can afford and that work for the project.

Seed Beads

These are the smallest beads. They come in donut, cylinder, and hexagon shapes. Mixing the shapes creates interesting texture. The smaller the size number, the bigger the bead. Size 11 is small; size 10 is bigger and easier to string (g).

E-beads

This is a great size and type of bead for embellishment work and can be threaded on colored cording. Plastic orange and green beads are strung on a double strand of orange Razzle™ thread by Wonderfil. Razzle is a rayon and metallic twist cord which is about equal to a size 8 crochet thread (h).

Bugle Beads

These are tube-shaped beads of different sizes and materials. They come in twisted shapes, too (i).

Novelty Beads

Collecting beads that look like fish, flowers, Santa Claus, or other novel shapes is great fun. Using them in your work is even better (j).

Buttons

To me a button is just a bead with several holes in it or with a shank on the back (k).

Beading Magazines and Books

Read about and look at the work of different bead artists and craftsmen for inspiration. Different artists go about using beads in different ways. Each has a point of view as to which techniques, threads, and types of beads are best. Each artist also has rules and tips unique to their own processes that can help us learn without making too many mistakes. How you work depends on your project and your point of view. There are beaders who only use the finest or most expensive beads; some prefer glass; some like acrylics and plastics; and some use everything.

Personally, I will mix anything that works for the design. I have even mixed semi-precious stone beads with the cheapest plastic beads to get the desired effect.

Bead Catalogs

My favorite catalog is from Fire Mountain Gems (see Resources on page 94). It is a veritable encyclopedia of beads with color pictures and descriptions of a huge variety. They are oriented toward the jewelry maker. The photos of finished projects are a rich source of inspiration for embellishment of fiber work. Just reading through the catalog is an education.

Online

I can spend hours in the evening surfing the Net to look at beads and the work of bead artists. I'll use search terms like "bead artist" and "art jewelry" and then use an image search. The wonderful work done today with beads is incredible and it is there for us to see. You can also find bead size charts and other technical information.

Experience Is the Best Teacher

With so many kinds of beads, the best way to learn about them is this: buy the ones you like and use them in your projects. You will understand more about the nature, effects, and purposes of the various sizes and types of beads by using them.

I will explain the beads as we go for each project. I'll tell you the type, size, and color of the beads I used. However, the size of the beads may vary in your project from mine, so be sure to measure your chosen bead mix to make sure it fits the project. Instead of specifying the number of beads on a string, for some of the projects I'll indicate the length of beads on the string.

You can choose to use the same beads as I've used or substitute what you prefer or what you have on hand. Use your favorite color schemes and fabrics for these projects to make them your own.

Bead Strings & Stitching Threads

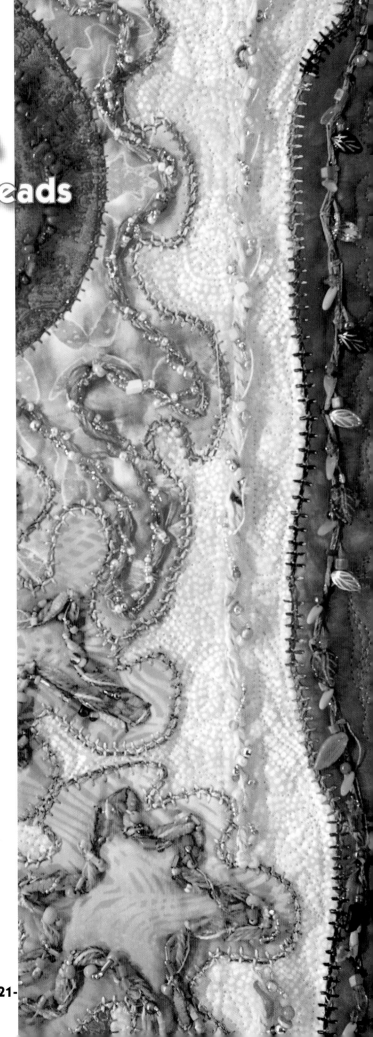

I just have to say this. Thank you, thread and yarn companies, for giving us such good quality, beautiful, and luscious fibers with which to work. Our needlework is possible and greatly enhanced because of your products!

The threads and yarns used in the projects in this book are chosen for several qualities. Beauty, strength, purpose, and function are all considerations. I understand that it is quite costly to buy all new threads, so I am suggesting the ones I consider best for the job. You can substitute with what you already have or what is available to you for these projects.

Understand that when a thread is in the center of the bead, environment and usage can affect the work. If you've ever seen an old beaded purse that is losing its beads, it is because cotton thread was used and over the years, moisture held by the beads has rotted the threads. If the project is a handbag or wearable, use strong thread so that if a bead catches on something, the thread won't break. A thread that stretches too much will eventually sag from the weight of the beads.

If you make an art quilt and the threads you choose are for aesthetics rather than strength, anchor the threads well and don't let people pull on the beads. (People shouldn't scrape paint off of oil paintings, either!)

Bead Strings

I call the thread used for stringing beads the "bead string." That is to differentiate it from the stitching thread that comes through the needle of the sewing machine.

The choice of bead string depends on several variables. The thread should be compatible with the size of the bead hole. You don't want a big bead wiggling around a fine thread; it won't hold the bead in place. On the other hand, if the thread is too thick, the beads won't string well.

I usually make the bead string twice the length of the beads strung on it. There must be enough bead string to secure it well to the work at the beginning and the end. The longest bead strings I make are 20" long. So, that is 10" of beads and 20" of string. It easier to handle this way.

For free-motion beading, the beads should be about one-fourth the length of the bead string. The extra string length gives you more options for stitching.

Cotton-Covered Polyester Thread

Cotton-covered polyester thread is produced by Coats & Clark and made for hand quilting. It is readily available and is what I have used for 30 years, first in my hand beading work and now with these techniques. It has a glazed finish so beads readily slip along the thread. It comes in many colors, is very strong, and doesn't stretch. It is easy to thread on a size 10 or 12 sharps needle, so seed beads string well on it. It has a polyester core, so I don't worry about the thread rotting. There is also no danger of melting under an iron because it is cotton and polyester, not nylon. It holds a secure knot because of the cotton covering.

Polyester Threads

In the past, the polyester threads I used were a little too stretchy and sometimes not very strong. I would use them anyway, especially the clear ones, if I wanted a shiny effect with transparent beads. Polyester threads, like all our threads, have greatly improved in the last few years.

Deco-Bob by WonderFil is a two-ply 80-weight polyester. It is extremely strong, doesn't stretch, and the tiniest beads string easily on it. It comes in many colors. I've tried different polyester threads and they work, but some stretch.

YLI Variations™ thread is a 35-weight trilobal polyester thread that comes in variegated shades. It is a very strong and pretty thread.

Cotton Threads

The threads in this category are strong and don't stretch. I have used them for bead strings, couching bead strings, and decorative stitching, all with success. I know that these makers take their threads very seriously and the quality is high. I will use the thread that is the right color and the right weight for my project. Different brands are more readily available in different parts of the country. I have included all the ones I use.

Silco by WonderFil is a 40-weight 100 percent cotton thread that comes in solid and variegated colors.

Superior Threads King Tut™ quilting thread is a 35-weight extra-long staple 100 percent Egyptian cotton. It comes in solid and variegated colors.

Sulky Blendables® thread is a long-staple, 100 percent Egyptian cotton in both 12- and

30-weight variegated colors. The 12 weight is especially good for bigger bead holes.

Machine Quilting Thread by YLI is a 40-weight cotton thread. These are great threads for medium and large beads. I will quadruple the threads to fit a larger bead hole. They are pretty and add to the decorative nature of the work.

Silamide and Nymo

Silamide is a pre-waxed nylon thread of twisted filaments. Nymo® beading thread is a lightly waxed nylon that threads easily and resists twisting and knotting. Many hand beaders and jewelry makers use these specialty threads. They are very strong threads, come in colors, and are perfect for their purpose. If you are strong believer in these threads, by all means use them for your bead strings.

I generally don't use clear nylon thread for the techniques in this book. If the sewing machine needle pierces the bead string, it will break the nylon thread whereas it will only split cotton-covered polyester. Ask me how I know!

Yarns and Other Fibers

Yarn can be used for bead string for beads with big holes and as decoration between the beads. Keep in mind that if the item gets wet, the yarn inside the beads will remain damp for a long time and potentially rot if it is cotton or rayon. I admit that I use anything to achieve the effect desired and don't worry if the work isn't going to last one hundred years.

The projects in this book use a variety of yarns for different effects. Look at the yarns you may have and see the possibilities for use.

Got Thread?

You may have a wonderful stash of threads from years of hand needlework. I have heard of people throwing out threads because somebody told them that they rot after a year. Really??? Museums and our attics are filled with textiles a lot older than that! Just do the "pull" test on your thread and see if it is still strong. If some threads have faded or yellowed over the years and they are still strong, then you have a variegated thread!

When a pattern calls for cording, a variety of fibers will work. Try gimp, tightly twisted or braided yarn, or crochet cotton. I've used them all and they all work well.

Other fibers to consider for machine bead work include:
- embroidery floss
- ribbon yarn
- novelty threads
- machine embroidery threads
- rayon

Ideas for Design

In bead work, the inspiration can come from any of three elements—fabric, beads, and yarn or thread—or an idea can inspire the gathering of these elements.

Here three sets of random bead mixes are strung and laid out with fabrics and yarns of similar colors. The mix of graphic designs in the fabric and the rough textured yarns make me think of architecture and old garden growth—seeds and forgotten little corners of a building or garden (a).

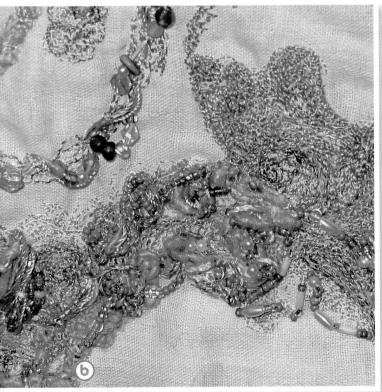

A sandy ocean shore is suggested by this mix. The fabric is creamy linen. The beads are made of pearls, glass, stones, and shells. Yarns include cotton and rayon crochet threads, nubby wool yarn, and creamy ribbon floss. All of these elements were thread painted with shiny rayon embroidery threads (b).

OPPOSITE PAGE: *This little work will become the cover of a box. The color inspiration came from a spool of Coats & Clark Star multicolor cotton.*

Turquoise and copper is a beautiful traditional color combination that can be the starting point for a project. These materials were gathered with this color combination in mind (c).

The work featured below has beads of wood, clay, seeds, and stones representing a forest floor (d).

The cutwork linen piece, shown on the opposite page, comes from Rust-Tex. When I saw this piece in Lois Jarvis' booth at a show, she suggested that it looked like a view through a window of a gathering storm or night sky. In this case, the fabric suggested the work and the beads are laid out to enhance the idea. This piece will be free-motion beaded (e).

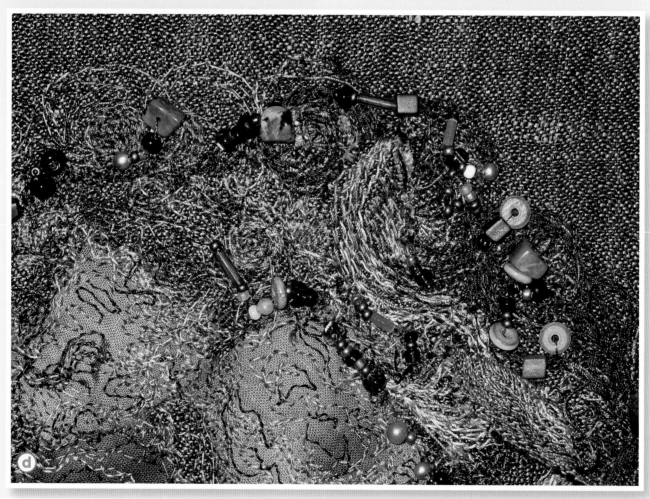

Other ideas for design sources include

Atmospheric debris—bugs, pollen, and rain suggested by a mix of beads of varied shapes, bugs, and flower-shaped beads

Ocean debris—tiny fish, plankton, bubbles, and sand suggested by a mix of pearls, glass, fish shapes, and seed beads

Bright graphics—a mix of plastic, clay, painted wooden discs, and glass beads

Architectural details—from castles or Victorian gingerbread houses, iron work, etc.

Patterning—patterns found in fabrics, papers, and wallpapers

Designing with Beads, Fabric, and Fiber

When designing with beads to be stitched on fabric, I work out the design of the beads on the fabric itself so I can see the effect of the colors.

Laying out every possible shape, size, and color of the beads I choose helps in the design process. A humble painted wooden bead is sometimes the perfect foil for a semi-precious stone or beautifully fired ceramic bead. When I use colored transparent beads, I consider the color of fabric showing through. One fabric can dull the bead while another may enhance it.

Step-by-Step Basic Techniques

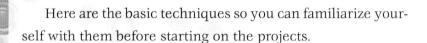

Here are the basic techniques so you can familiarize yourself with them before starting on the projects.

Make a test sample of each technique using cotton fabric, a medium-weight stabilizer, and beads as indicated. You can always recover the beads by cutting them out of your test samples.

Getting Started

All seven of the techniques start the same way.

Select your bead string thread. The thread should be comparable to the size of the bead holes.

Tie the first bead onto the end of the thread with a knot. (A simple knot in the thread is not big enough to hold the beads on the stringing thread.) Thread the bead string thread onto a beading needle and string the number of beads indicated onto the bead string.

Anchor the bead string to the fabric with three stitches in place, bring the needle under these stitches three more times, then make a knot. I have found this to be a very secure technique that doesn't loosen over time.

When a line of stitching is done, cut the knotted bead at the end of the bead string, pull off any extra beads, rethread the bead string, and secure with several stitches and a knot as at the beginning.

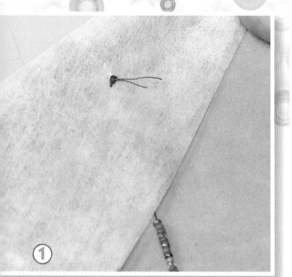

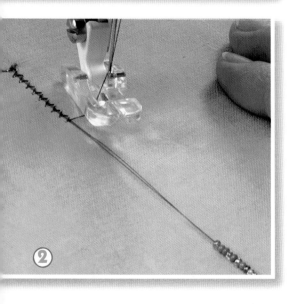

#1 Raindrops

Setup

Machine Setup

Use a beading foot.

Set your machine to a zigzag stitch.

Beading Setup

String 7" of seed beads onto an 18" length of thread.

The Beadle is used in this technique.

Technique

1. Secure the bead string to the fabric.

2. Couch with a zigzag stitch over the bead string for an inch.

3. * Pull the bead string to the side and zigzag stitch for an inch.

4. Bring the bead string back over the line of stitching and with the Beadle, scoot a few beads behind the needle and hold them in place.

5. Zigzag stitch forward over the bead string for an inch.

6. Repeat the process from the *.

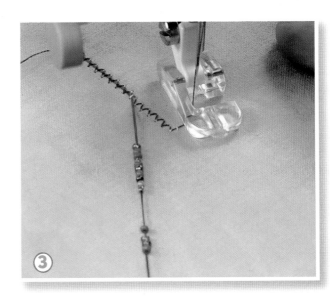

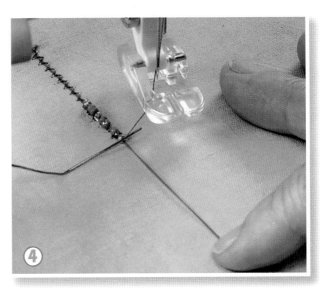

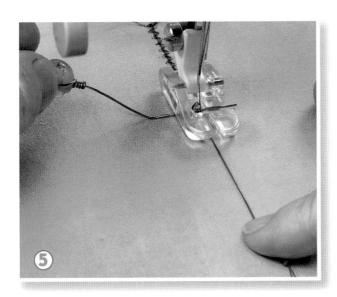

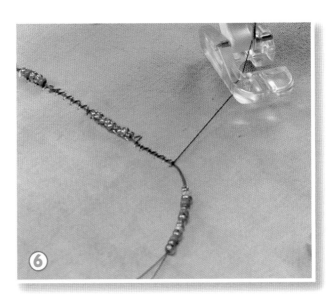

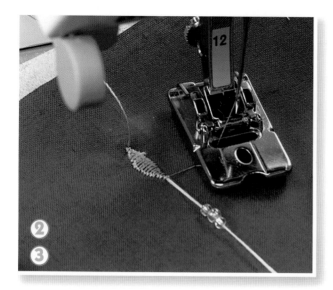

#2 Decorative Stitch

Setup

Machine Setup

Use a beading foot.

Set your machine to a decorative stitch that only goes forward. (You don't want to back up over a bead!)

Beading Setup

String 4" of E-beads onto an 18" length of thread.

The Beadle is used in this technique.

Technique

① Secure the bead string to the fabric. See Step 1 photo, page 28.

② Stitch one pattern of the decorative stitch over the bead string.

③ * Bring the sewing machine needle up and presser foot up. Move the fabric past the needle.

④ Scoot a few beads behind the needle with the Beadle. Hold the beads behind the needle.

⑤ Stitch another repeat of the decorative stitch over the bead string.

⑥ Repeat the process from the *.

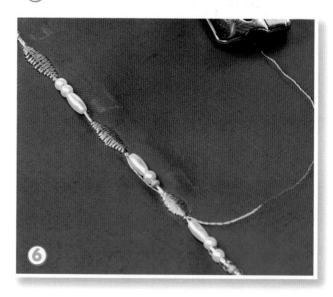

#3 Bar-Tack Yarn and Bead Wrap

Setup

Machine Setup

Take the foot off of your machine and use the ankle only. (Note: I'm using a Bernina® sewing machine and the ankle is attached to the foot. I used the ankle that came with my Creative Feet for this technique.)

Set your machine to a bar-tack or a zig-zag stitch with the widest setting and set the length at .5.

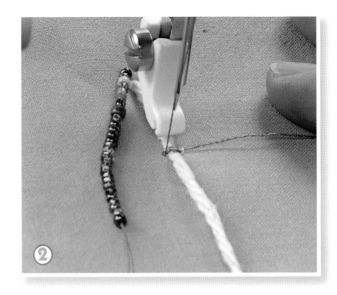

Beading Setup

String 7" of a bead mix onto an 18" length of thread.

Cut an 18" length of a thick and nubby yarn.

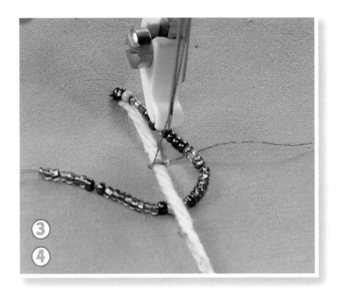

Technique

① Secure both the yarn and the bead string to the fabric. See Step 1 photo, page 28.

② Stitch one bar-tack over the yarn only.

③ Wrap the bead string around the yarn once.

④ Bring needle and presser foot up. Even though there is no presser foot on the machine, this action is necessary to release the thread tension so that you can move the work.

⑤ Move the fabric about an inch from the bar-tack. Bar-tack only the yarn.

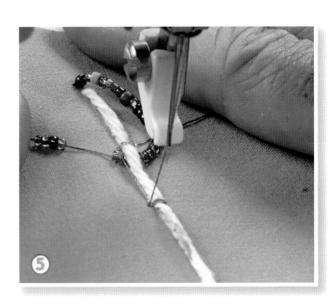

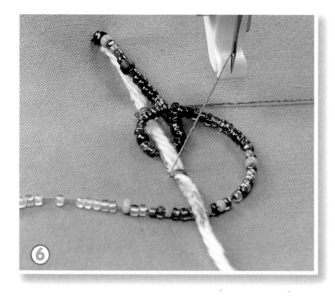

(6) * Wrap the bead string around the yarn once. Move the fabric another inch from the bar-tack.

(7) Bar-tack the yarn only. Repeat the process from the *.

#4 Couch Bead String and Pull

This is the easiest thing in the world to do. You create a casing or tunnel through which the bead string is pulled through taut. The zigzag stitch couches over the bead string, stitching into the fabric and not the string. The zigzag stitch creates the casing. It is essential that you don't get the bead string caught in the stitches.

Use a foot that will help you see the center point of the stitch. An appliqué foot is the best choice. As long as you keep the bead string at center needle position, the bead string will remain in the center of the stitch and the stitch will clear the string.

Setup

Machine Setup

Use an open-toed appliqué foot if you have it, otherwise use a zigzag presser foot.

Set your machine to a wide zigzag stitch.

Beading Setup

String 7" of mixed beads onto a single strand of cord or a doubled or tripled thread 18" long.

Technique

(1) Secure the bead string to the fabric. See Step 1 photo, page 28.

(2) Using a wide zigzag, stitch over the bead string for about an inch, being careful not to stitch into the cord.

(3) *Pull several beads up along the bead string, hold them to the side, and measure the span they cover. Place a mark on the fabric indicating the length of the beads. Stitch to the mark with the beads and bead string still looped to the side.

(4) Bring the bead string back to the line of stitching. Hold the beads behind the foot and stitch over the cord for another inch.

(5) Repeat the process from the *.

(6) When the line of stitching is finished, pull on the remaining bead string, shortening it so that the beads pop into place.

Use this method to attach large beads or shank buttons.

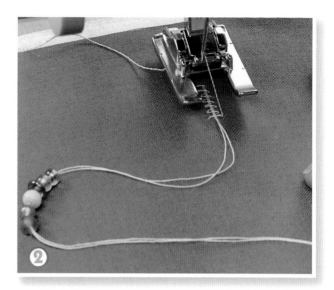

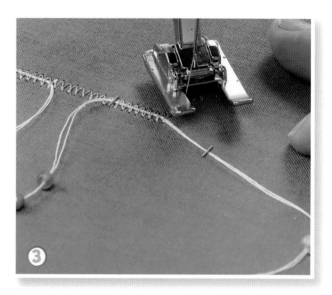

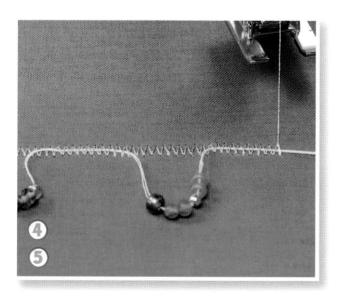

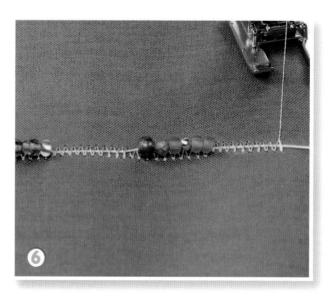

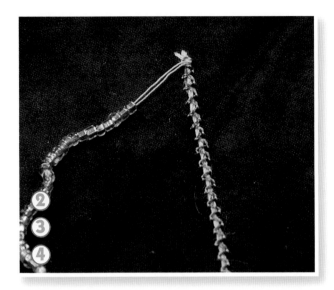

#5 Loop Fringe

Setup

Machine Setup

Use an open-toed appliqué foot if you have it, otherwise use a zigzag presser foot.

Set your machine to a small zigzag stitch.

Beading Setup

String 8" of seed beads onto an 18" length of thread.

Cut a piece of pearl cotton or decorative cording 10" long.

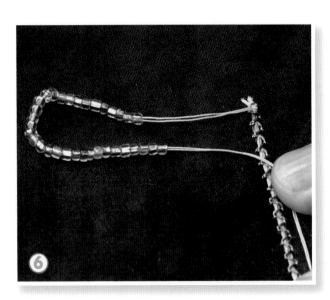

Technique

① Secure the decorative cording to the fabric by pulling it through to the back of the fabric and making a knot.

② Couch the decorative cording to the fabric.

③ Secure the bead string right next to the beginning of the cording.

④ Bar-tack the bead string next to the cording.

⑤ Measure 2" of beads.

⑥ Form a loop with the 2" length of beads.

(7) Bar-tack the bead string next to the first bar-tack.

(8) *Zigzag stitch over the bead string next to the cording for about ½".

(9) Bar-tack over the bead string.

(10) Measure and loop 2" of beads and bar-tack the bead string next to the last bar-tack.

Repeat the process from the * until the fringe is finished.

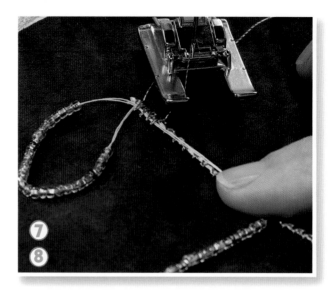

#6 Free-Motion Beading

Setup

Machine Setup

Use an open-toed free-motion or darning foot. If you don't have this, you may stitch with only the ankle.

Set the sewing machine to straight stitch, drop the feed dogs, and lower the upper thread tension. (If you don't know how to do free-motion embroidery, there is a pretty good AQS book on the subject—*Thread Painting Made Easy,* by Terry White!)

Beading Setup

String 8" of a bead mix onto an 18" length of thread.

The Beadle is used in this technique.

Hoop the fabric and stabilizer.

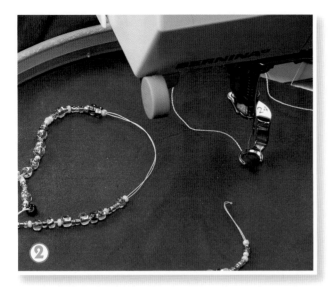

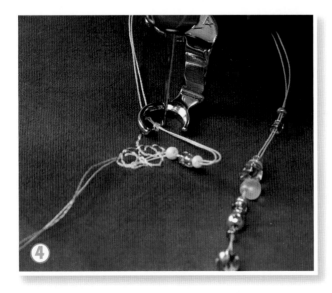

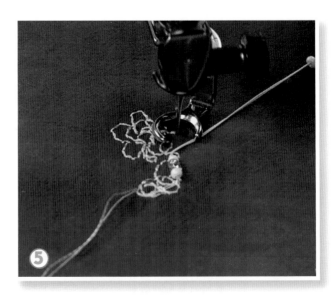

Technique

(1) Secure the bead string to the hooped fabric. See Step 1 photo, page 28.

(2) Position the hoop under the needle.

(3) Do some free-motion stitching, ending with the needle about ½" away from the bead string.

*Using the Beadle, pull some beads along the bead string, and pull the bead string toward the needle.

(4) Stitch over the bead string not catching it, while holding the beads away from the needle with the Beadle. Pull the bead string so the beads pop into place.

(5) Do some more free-motion stitching over the bead string, then stitch away from the bead string.

(6) Repeat the process from the *.

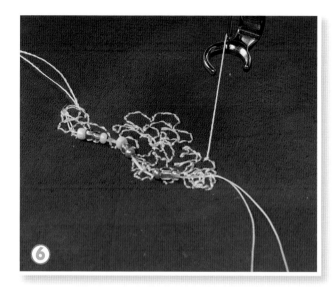

#7 Seed Bead Fill

This is a technique that requires practice to do good work. The design of the cuff bracelet project that uses this technique is simple for that reason. Practice on scrap fabrics. You can always recover the beads by cutting them out of unsuccessful tries.

Each time you practice, you will understand a little better where to end the line of beads in a design, how to be consistent, which thread tension works the best, etc.

Setup

Machine Setup

Remove the foot and use only the ankle.

Set sewing machine to a straight stitch, drop the feed dogs, and lower the thread tension.

Heart trinket box with bead fill

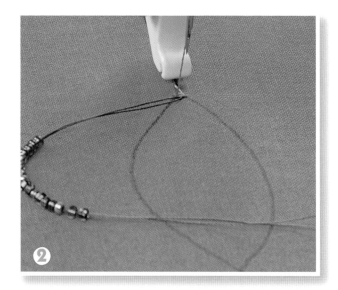

Beading Setup

String 8" of seed beads onto an 18" length of thread.

The Beadle is used in this technique.

Hoop the fabric and stabilizer.

Technique

(1) Draw a simple leaf shape on the fabric. Secure the bead string to the hooped fabric. See the Step 1 photo, page 28.

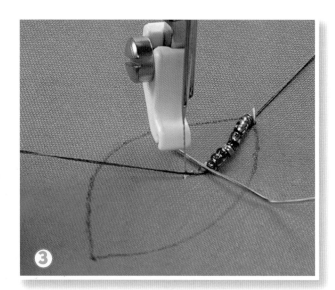

(2) Position the hoop under the needle. Start at the tip of the leaf. Take a few small stitches back and forth over the bead string.

(3) Stitch about ½" line of stitching along the center of the design. Pull about ½" of the beads along the string and hold them in place with the Beadle. Stitch over the bead string, almost like a little bar-tack.

(4) Stitch down about ½". Pull ½" of beads down the bead string with the Beadle and hold in place while stitching over the bead string.

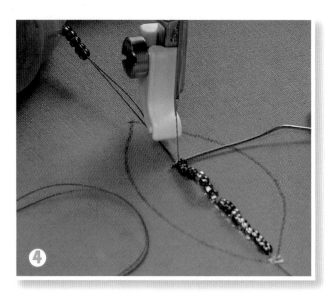

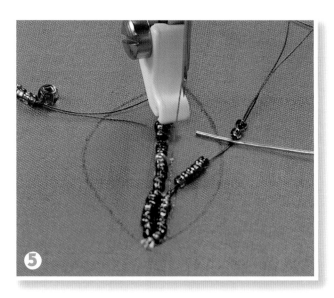

⑤ Work back and forth in this manner, stitching down the bead string, ½" of beads at a time. Keep lines of beads very close to fill in the area.

⑥ Cover the bead string ends by stitching decoratively around the bead-filled shapes.

Fill shapes can vary, as can the way any given shape is filled, as you can see in these examples.

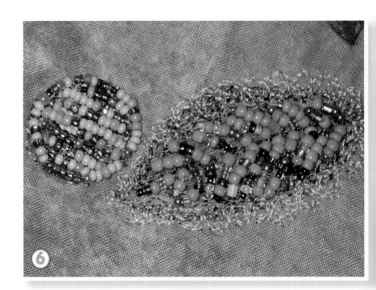

Quilting Beaded Work

Lay the beaded top onto the batting and backing and baste the layers together. Take big tacking stitches about 4" apart over the quilt top with hand quilting thread. I like this better than pin basting because it doesn't distort the layers as pins can. I'm not crazy about adding adhesive to my work, so I don't use a fabric adhesive spray.

A standard free-motion quilting foot can get caught on or break the beads. Take the foot off your machine but leave the ankle. This gives some stabilization to the quilting without interfering with the beads. If your machine feet don't come apart like this, you can order a snap-on adapter from Creative Feet (see Resources, page 94).

RAIN DANCE, *13½" x 21½", made by the author*

RAIN DANCE

This fantasy flower patch is appliquéd, embellished with beads, and quilted.

Techniques

Bead by Machine **Technique #1 – Raindrops** (page 29)

Bead clusters – a simple and effective embellishment idea. I am bound to tell you that I had to sneak this hand technique in the book. However, it is fun to do and perfect for this quilt.

Supplies

Fabrics

- ⑥ 12" x 18" blue cotton for background
- ⑥ 2 strips 2½" x 13½" deep coral print for top and bottom borders
- ⑥ 2 strips 1½" x 18" light coral print for side borders
- ⑥ ⅛ yard deep coral for flower petals and border ovals
- ⑥ 1 square 6" x 6" purple for clouds
- ⑥ ⅛ yard multicolor print for cloud and flower mound
- ⑥ ⅛ yard yellow green for leaves and border squares
- ⑥ scraps of medium green for leaves and grass
- ⑥ scraps of yellow for flower centers
- ⑥ 15" x 24" rectangle for backing

Tools & Notions

- ⑥ 17" x 26" rectangle batting (I used 60/40 by Fairfield)
- ⑥ 2 yards ½" wide ribbon yarn for binding
- ⑥ 17" x 26" rectangle nonwoven, medium weight interfacing
- ⑥ 1 yard fusible web
- ⑥ beading foot
- ⑥ The Beadle

Thread

- ⑥ Deco Bob for quilting
- ⑥ transparent polyester thread or Sulky transparent blue metallic #142-7044 for raindrops bead string and stitching
- ⑥ YLI Variations polyester thread for bead clusters:
    - ⑥ light blue for cloud bead clusters
    - ⑥ orange for leaf bead clusters
    - ⑥ yellow/orange variegated cotton thread for orange bead string and stitching
- ⑥ rayon machine embroidery threads for appliqué stitching:
    - ⑥ light green
    - ⑥ pale blue
    - ⑥ purple

supplies continued

Beads

- Gather beads comparable to the ones I used (a).
- **Top row:** orange glass leaf beads with pink and green E-beads for the leaf clusters
- **Second row:** glass flower bead, iridescent light blue E-beads, and blue tri-beads for the flower clusters
- **Third row:** seed beads (already strung) for the rain drops including varied sizes and colors, mostly light, and a mix of iridescent and transparent glass beads
- **Bottom row:** orange E-bead mix (already strung)

Making Rain Dance

Sew the borders to the blue background, starting with the sides.

Trace the appliqué designs, (pages 46–48), onto fusible web and place onto the back of the fabrics. Fuse and cut out shapes according to manufacturer's directions. Place the squares and ovals around the border (See photo on page 40).

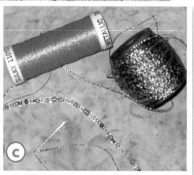

Position the stabilizer under the background and stitch around all the pieces with a tiny zigzag stitch using a 40-weight rayon machine embroidery thread. Use orange variegated cotton to stitch the border squares and ovals with a large zigzag stitch (b).

Beading the Raindrops

String the raindrop beads with a thread twice as long as you need for the row, knotting the first bead onto the end. I used a shiny multicolor polyester-core metallic from Japan (something that I found at a fancy fiber booth at a quilt show). A good substitute is a polyester core metallic by Sulky, #142-7044. Its iridescence adds to the rainy effect (c).

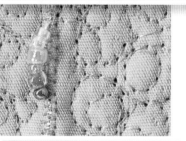

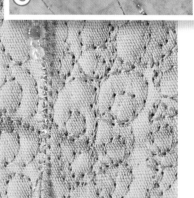

Anchor the bead string at the top of the first raindrop line.

Thread the machine with the Sulky blue metallic and set to a zigzag stitch.

Stitch over the bead string for about ½" (d).

Move the bead string to the side of the stitching. Stitch forward another ½", being sure to clear the bead string.

Leave the needle down and bring the presser foot up. Align the bead string over the line of zigzag stitching.

Scoot ½" of seed beads behind the needle with the Beadle and hold them in place under the presser foot (e).

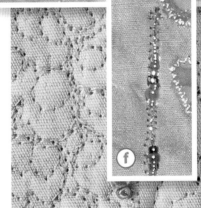

Lower the presser foot and stitch forward ½".

Repeat this process until the row is finished (f).

Cut the knotted bead off the end and remove any remaining beads from the bead string.

Thread the bead string onto a hand needle and pull to the back of the work. Secure the end of the bead string the same way you secured the beginning.

Bead the remaining lines of raindrops the same way.

Beading the Borders

String 9" of orange beads on a 30" length of yellow/orange variegated cotton thread for the side borders.

String 6" of orange beads on a 20" length of yellow/orange variegated cotton thread for the top and bottom.

Thread your machine with the same thread as the bead string.

Zigzag stitch over the bead string in the spaces between the ovals. Position the orange beads over the ovals (g).

Orange Leaf Clusters

It's times like this that I figure out why I buy things like orange leaf beads (h). I probably thought they were pretty and knew someday I would use them. I can't even remember where or when I acquired them. It doesn't matter, they are perfect for this quilt!

I placed the orange leaf beads on the quilt and scattered them around the flowers until I liked the placement. Then I used an orange permanent pen to indicate where they would go when I was ready to stitch them down. This really helps because it is hard to remember exactly where you placed them.

The orange leaves will be stitched down as a bead cluster (yes, I slipped in a hand-stitching technique).

Thread a 10 or 12 sharps needle with 18" of orange Variations polyester thread by YLI .

Secure the thread on the back where you want the bead cluster (i).

Come through to the front, string 3 pink E-beads and 3 leaf beads. Then simply put the needle back into the fabric very close to where you came out, pull to the back, forming the cluster, and secure the thread (j).

Flower Cloud Bead Clusters

In the same way, scatter some flower-shaped beads among the clouds until you're happy with their placement. Mark the position for each flower cluster with a marking pen.

Thread a 10 or 12 sharps needle with 18" of light blue YLI Variations polyester thread.

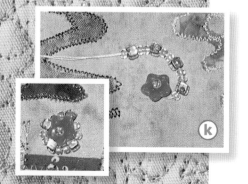

String and hand stitch a flower bead stacked with a seed bead. Then string 4 seed beads and wrap them around the flower bead. It is essentially the same technique as sewing the orange leaf clusters, but hand tack the cluster in two places between the beads before securing the thread on the back (k).

Quilting

Layer the beaded top with the batting and backing and baste.

I machine quilted small circular motifs in the blue area of the quilt and around the small appliqué shapes, leaving them raised. I quilted on the leaves and around the yellow flower centers for added definition. The borders were quilted with straight lines (l).

For the binding, I stitched ribbon yarn a scant ¼" along the edge of the back. Then, I brought it around to the front of the work and used a big machine blanket stitch to fasten it to the front (m).

Appliqué pattern

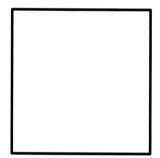

Make 16 squares.

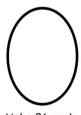

Make 26 ovals.

Appliqué pattern

Appliqué pattern

ALL BEADED UP BY MACHINE ○ TERRY WHITE

RED ONION CROSSHATCH BAG, *18" x 18", made by the author*

Red Onion Crosshatch Bag

The simple crosshatch technique adds texture to a stenciled surface design. The bead string is a somewhat stiff variegated gimp from the Painter's Palette, carried by YLI threads. It adds extra texture and dimension to the beads.

Techniques

Bead by Machine **Technique #2 – Decorative Stitch** (page 30)

Couching using a cording foot

Supplies

Fabric

- 11" x 11" square of gold linen
- ¾ yard of striped fabric for the front of the bag and handle
- 1 fat quarter patterned fabric for the back of the bag
- ½ yard lining
- ⅛ yard purple cotton for ragged piping trim

Tools & Notions

- medium-weight nonwoven interfacing for stabilizer
- stencil plastic
- red fabric paint
- stencil brush
- The Beadle

Thread

- variegated orange/red gimp, yarn, or several strands of pearl cotton
- King Tut™ cotton variegated reds

Beads

- 115 terra cotta 4mm x 3mm square beads (a)
- 35 purple 4mm x 3mm square beads (a)

Making the Red Onion Panel

Trace the red onion design (page 53) onto stencil plastic and cut out.

Stencil 4 onions on gold linen with red fabric paint and a stencil brush, following the manufacturer's instructions for drying and setting (b).

Place a piece of stabilizer behind the onion panel. Center on a 20" x 20" square of background fabric (c).

Thread the machine with thread that matches the linen.

Stitch around the edges of the panel with a zigzag stitch. The background fabric will act as extra stabilizer.

Use a water-soluble marking pen to draw a grid of diagonal lines ¾" apart, starting with a line going from one corner to the opposite corner of the panel (d).

Thread the machine with King Tut variegated red thread. Use a serpentine decorative stitch to couch the red gimp down one set of diagonals (e).

Count the intersections on each line to determine how many beads to string for each line. String a purple bead at the beginning and end of each row. String the square beads on the gimp and stitch them down on the other set of diagonal lines, positioning each bead at an intersection, using the same serpentine decorative stitch between each intersection (f).

To finish the edge of the onion panel, stitch a second row of zigzag stitches around the edge of the panel, catching the ends of the gimp. This stabilizes the panel. The gimp is not pulled to the back as it can distort the fabric.

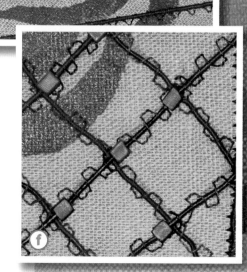

Cut ¾" wide strips of a contrasting fabric (purple).

Using a cording foot and a wide zigzag stitch, couch the strip along the edge of the onion panel, extending about 1½" beyond each corner. Stitch a second time for a "stitchier" look (g).

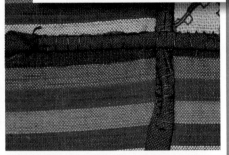

Making the Bag

Trim the onion panel to measure 18" square.

Sew an 18" x 18" square of fabric for the back of the bag to the bottom of the front panel, right sides together.

Stitch the side seams of the bag, right sides together.

Cut a piece of lining fabric 18" x 34". Fold in half, right sides together, and stitch the side seams.

From the wrong side and at the bottom corners, flatten out the points of the lining. Draw a line 1½" from the point. Stitch on this line. Do not trim the corners. The extra fabric will add to the strength of the bag (h).

Do the same for the inside corners of the bag.

Fold under ¼" along the top edge. Press.

Fold the top edge of both the bag and the lining another 1" and press.

Put the lining in the bag, wrong sides together, matching up the inside corners. Pin the top edges together (i).

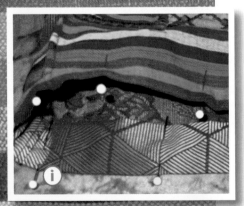

Making the Handle

Cut a 3" strip across the width of the striped fabric.

Press in the long edges a scant 1". Fold the length in half, encasing the raw edges, and blanket stitch along both edges (j).

Pin the handle in place at the sides of the bag between the bag and the lining. Stitch around the top of the bag with a large blanket stitch, stitching the handle in place. Stitch around the top several more times with the blanket stitch for a "stitchier" look. Then stitch an X in a box to reinforce the end of the handles (k). Sew another row of blanket stitches 1" down from the top edges to secure the inside hem of the bag and add another line of decorative stitch on the outside of the bag.

Lay the bag flat. Tuck in the sides and fold up the bottom the way a paper bag is folded. Press, then pin the pressed edges (l).

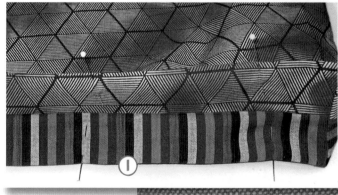

Stitch a blanket stitch along the pressed edges of the front and back of the bag (m).

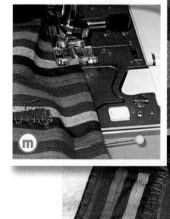

Stencil pattern

DIVA BOX TOP, *7" x 9", made by the author*

Diva Box Top

A textural and complex striped pattern is created with couched cording, rows of background stitching, and beads—all done with decorative stitches.

Techniques

Bead by Machine **Technique #1— Raindrops** (page 29)

Bead by Machine **Technique #2— Decorative Stitch** (page 30)

Couching

Supplies

Fabric

⑥ 15" x 15" square pink 100 percent cotton in a textured print

Tools & Notions

⑥ 15" x 15" square of medium-weight non-woven interfacing
⑥ water-soluble marking pen
⑥ cording foot
⑥ open-toed embroidery foot
⑥ beading foot
⑥ fabric glue
⑥ The Beadle tool was invented for this technique!

Thread

⑥ pink metallic machine embroidery thread
⑥ peach metallic machine embroidery thread
⑥ pink variegated cotton
⑥ black variegated cotton
⑥ rose color rayon machine embroidery thread
⑥ pink rayon machine embroidery thread
⑥ black cotton thread

Yarn

⑥ pink silk
⑥ brown and dusty pink worsted weight crochet cotton

Beads

⑥ black, pink, lilac, and copper E-beads up to ¼" (a)
⑥ random mix of seed beads
⑥ 4 buttons for the corners

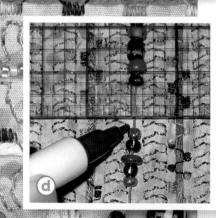

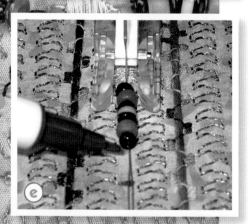

Making the Diva Box Top

Draw a rectangle the finished size of your box top on the fabric, then a series of straight horizontal lines 1" apart. See the stitching diagram on page 58. Keep in mind that the stitching will shrink the cloth a bit.

Put the cording foot on your machine. Place the interfacing under the fabric and couch yarns along the horizontal lines with a decorative stitch and variegated thread (b).

Change to an open-toed embroidery foot and add rows of decorative stitches between the couched cording. Use two threads through the eye of the sewing machine needle to add color and weight to the stitch. A rose rayon thread and peach metallic were used with this decorative stitch (c).

Make 3 bead strings with an ordered arrangement of 6" of E-beads on an 18" length of thread.

Lay the bead string between the rows of decorative stitches to check the bead placement. This will help you decide the size of the decorative stitch to use.

After stitching a few samples, I found that the oval satin stitch was the right size for my project. It is a little smaller than ½". This gave me a little wiggle room for my beads. I used two threads through the eye of the needle—a variegated pink cotton and a solid pink rayon.

Use a water-soluble marking pen to indicate the start of each bead group so their placement will be uniform (d).

Change to the pearls and piping foot. Secure the bead string in the work at the top of the line. Stitch one decorative stitch. Scoot the first group of beads up to measure where the next stitch should be and mark that spot (e).

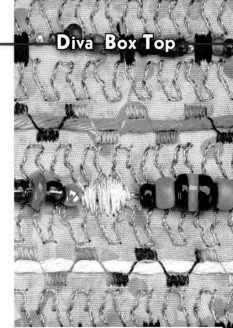

Pull the bead string away from the center line.

With needle up and presser foot up, position the needle over the stitch mark. Take a few stitches in place. Pull the bead string back in the line of stitching and hold the beads in place with the Beadle. Lower the presser foot. The beads should fit into the groove on the bottom of the foot. Stitch over the bead string to the next start mark.

Continue in this manner to stitch the 3 arranged bead strings.

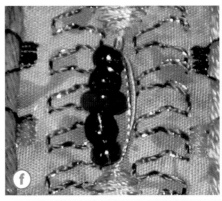

The top thread will jump between decorative stitches and lie along the side of the bead group (f).

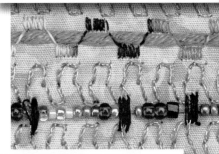

You can leave this as an additional decorative element or trim it. If you fix the beginning and end of each decorative stitch, you can snip this off. If you don't have the fix capability on your machine, you can add a little glue to the back of the work at these points so that the stitches don't unravel.

Make 4 bead strings in a random arrangement with 6" of seed beads on an 18" length of thread.

Secure the bead string at the beginning of the line. Using black cotton thread, bar-tack the bead string with a wide zigzag stitch.

Bring the needle and presser foot up. Move the work forward for about ½". Scoot the beads behind the needle with the Beadle and bar-tack over the bead string (g).

Continue in this manner until the end of the bead string and secure the string at the end.

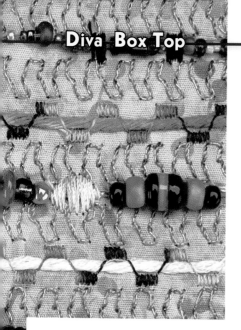

The black bar-tack almost looks like a bead. I stitched inconsistent lengths of zigzag stitches for a more informal appearance.

Compare the size of the beaded area to the size of your box top. Fold under the edges to fit and stitch additional rows of decorative stitches or corded yarn to finish the edges.

Hand stitch the buttons to the corners and secure the panel to your box top with fabric glue.

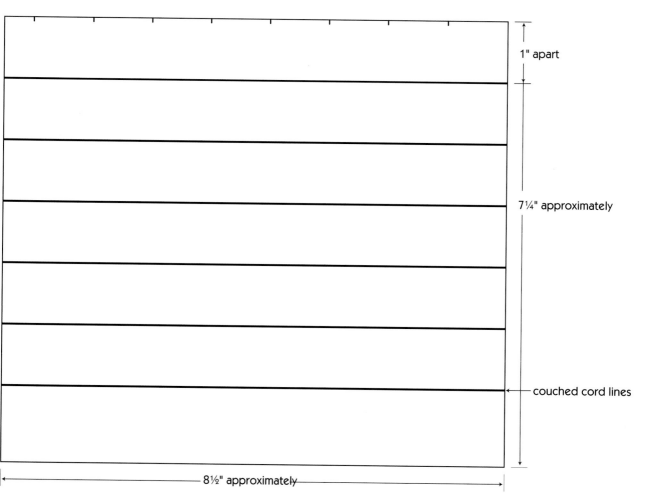

1" apart

7¼" approximately

couched cord lines

8½" approximately

Stitching diagram for Diva Box Top

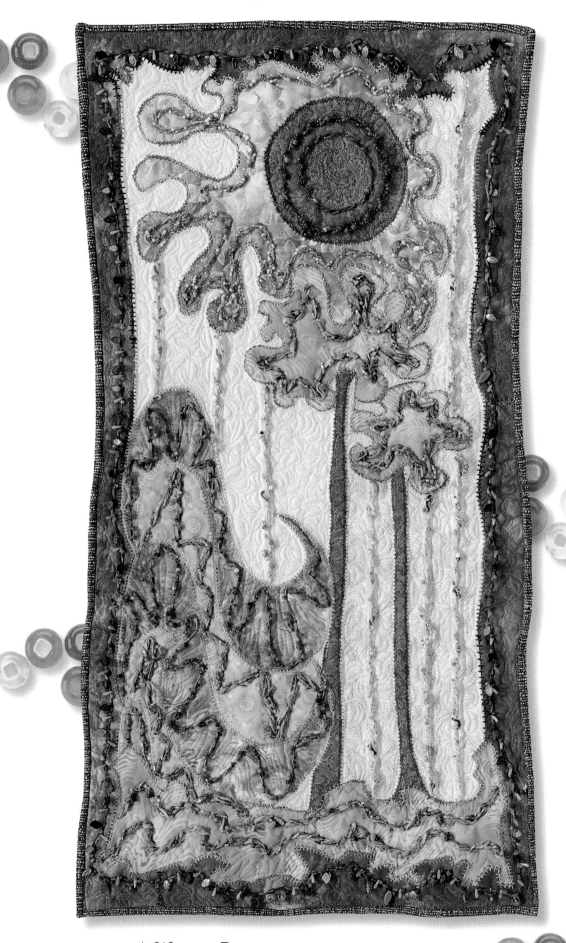

A Winter's Daydream, *17" x 33", made by the author*

A Winter's Daydream

Bright color cottons were used for the shapes in this wall quilt. This is not an appliqué project in the usual sense of the word. The pieces are cut out and laid edge-to-edge on a fusible interfacing like a jigsaw puzzle, then fused with a hot iron. Decorative machine stitches join the edges of the shapes and stitch them to the interfacing at the same time

To keep the weight of the beads from distorting this quilt, you'll add the batting to the quilt top before doing the beading.

Technique

Bead by Machine **Technique #3—Bar-Tack Yarn and Bead Wrap** (page 31)

Supplies

Fabric

- ¼ yard each light yellow, medium yellow, blue, light green, medium green, red
- ⅓ yard lavender
- fat quarter of orangey-pink
- ⅝ yard for the backing
- ¼ yard for the binding

Tools & Notions

- 20" x 36" nonwoven medium-weight fusible interfacing
- 1 pkg. half-inch iron-on seam tape
- cording: 5 yards each dark lavender, green, and red; 4 yards blue; 3 yards pink
- cording foot
- 21" x 37" batting
- The Beadle

Thread

- 30-weight rayon machine embroidery threads for the bead strings that blend with the 8 fabrics

Yarn

- several yards of 3 different yarns or ribbons in each of the 8 fabric colors

Beads

- approximately 6 ounces (170 grams) color-specific random bead mixes in each of the 8 fabric colors

The shapes of the beads don't matter. They range in size from #10 seed beads to beads approximately 8 mm—all different sizes but in the same color family.

Here are the fabrics, threads, yarns, and beads laid out together for this project. Gathering these treasures (I mean supplies) is part of the creative process. Even though all of these things weren't used in the final project, the grouping of everything was the inspiration for the quilt (a).

Making the Quilt

Starch the fabrics and trace the shapes onto the appropriate color fabrics. Do not reverse the patterns. Use a light box or tape the patterns to a sunny window and trace.

Cut out the shapes and lay them on the fusible interfacing. They fit together like puzzle pieces. Press with a hot iron. Don't worry if the shapes don't fit exactly, but get them as tightly fitted as you can (b).

Thread the machine with thread to match your cording. Use a cording foot to couch around all the shapes, joining the edges and stitching the pieces to the interfacing at the same time (c).

Place the quilt top on batting only. Baste the two layers together with a tack stitch.

Machine Setup for Beading

ankle only (remove foot)

feed dogs down

For each area to be beaded, loosely twist 20" strands of 3 different yarns or ribbons in the same color as the area to be beaded. Several sets of yarn and beads will be used in some areas (d). (For example, 5 bead strings were used in the sun's aura.)

Thread the strand through a tapestry needle, bring it to the back, and knot it. Trim the ends to 1" and press a 1" piece of iron-on seam tape over the ends to keep them from interfering with the stitching (e).

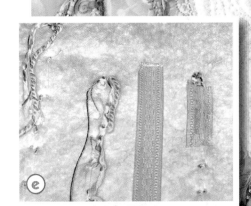

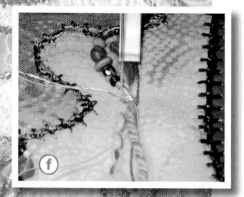

String 10" of beads on a 20" bead string.

Anchor the bead string at the top of the yarn strand. Pull about ½" of beads to the top of the bead string (f). Hold in place with the Beadle and bar-tack over the bead string and the yarns with a wide zigzag stitch (g).

Raise the needle and presser foot. Bring the needle forward about an inch. Slide another ½" of beads up the bead string and twist around the yarns. Bar-tack over the bead string and the yarns. Continue in this manner (h).

When one bead string comes to an end, secure the end and remove any extra beads. Start in the same place with another bead string to finish the row.

The photos below show the yarn and bead mixes and how they look with the fabrics (i).

Add the backing fabric and quilt the work.

Cut 2" wide strips for the binding. Fold in half lengthwise and machine stitch to the back of the quilt, aligning the raw edges. Turn to the front of the quilt and finish with a decorative stitch.

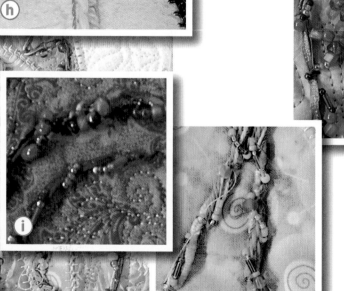

Appliqué pattern, *enlarge 400%*

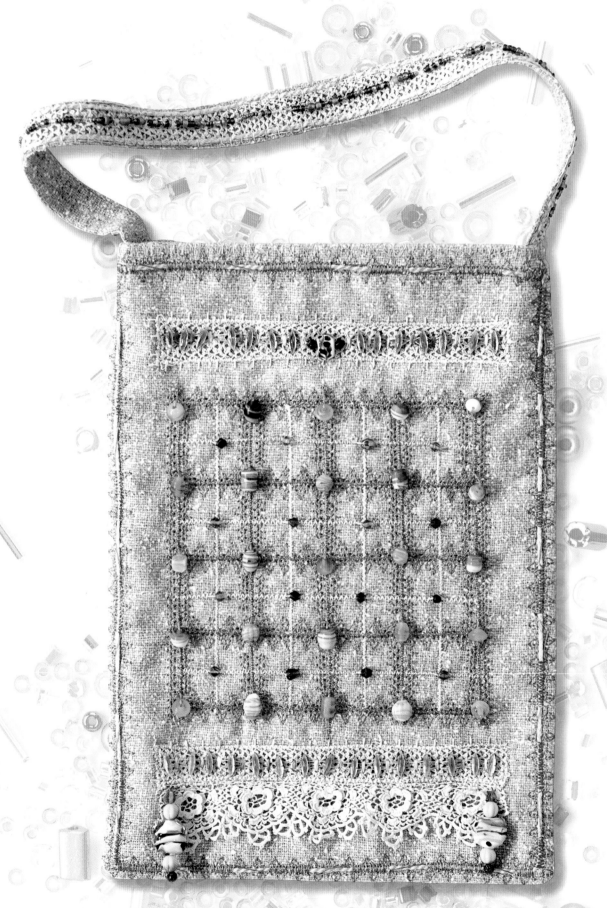

Vintage Jewel Bag, *9" x 12", made by the author*

ALL BEADED UP BY MACHINE ○ TERRY WHITE

Vintage Jewel Bag

The mixed textures of the materials in this simple project make it interesting. Unique handmade glass beads and vintage hand crocheted trims work with coarse linen and mismatched beads in a natural color palette. If you don't have old lace, there are many beautiful machine-made laces on the market today. Look in the bridal section of fabric stores for gorgeous rayon laces.

With so many one-of-a-kind elements, it would be practically impossible for you to recreate this handbag exactly. That is good. Use your own personal treasures to make yours unique.

Techniques

Bead by Machine **Technique #1 — Raindrops** (page 29)

Bead by Machine **Technique #3 — Bar-Tack variation** (page 31)

Couching

Supplies

Fabrics

- ½ yard coarse natural color linen cut as follows:
    - 2 pieces 15" x 18" for the front and back
    - 1 strip 2" x 18" for handle
- ½ yard dusty pink polyester drapery fabric (mimics silk dupioni)

Tools & Notions

- 3 pieces of 1"–1½" wide lace 7" long
- 1 piece of 1"–1½" lace 18" long for the handle
- ½ yard nonwoven stabilizer
- ½ yard half-inch Steam-A-Seam® fusible tape
- cording foot
- open-toed embroidery foot
- The Beadle

Yarn

- rayon cording in coral and yellow for bead strings
- twisted sage green rayon yarn for border

Thread

- 30-weight lilac rayon machine embroidery thread
- 30-weight yellow and coral rayon machine embroidery threads
- 50-weight cotton variegated yellow/pink/purple thread

supplies continued

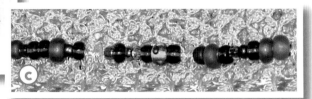

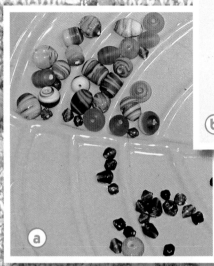

Beads

- ✆ 25 half-inch mismatched natural color beads for center panel (a)
- ✆ 16 quarter-inch beads of dark amber and purple for the center panel (a)
- ✆ mix of large glass beads for the bead drops (b)
- ✆ pale pink glass beads in 2-hole settings (b)
- ✆ mix of E-beads in natural colors for the handle (c)

Decorative Stitching

Draw the lines of the grid in the center of a 15" x 18" piece of linen with a water-soluble pen. Add stabilizer to the back.

Thread your machine with lilac rayon embroidery thread and sew rows of decorative stitches on both sides of the 5 vertical and 5 horizontal solid lines (d).

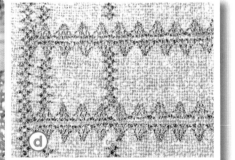

Change to a cording foot and couch yellow rayon cording with a small zigzag stitch directly over the vertical dashed lines, between the double rows of decorative stitching (e).

Stitch Bead String

String 4 quarter-inch beads on an 18" length of yellow rayon cording.

Change to an open-toed embroidery foot.

Secure the bead string at the end of a horizontal dashed line.

Stitch over the bead string with a small zigzag and stop several stitches before intersecting with a vertical couched line, then move the bead string away from the line of stitching (f).

Stitch a few stitches over the intersection and beyond. With needle and presser foot up, scoot a bead behind the needle and hold in position with the Beadle so the bead doesn't jump forward (g).

Reposition the bead string over the dashed line, lower the presser foot, and stitch to just before the next intersection. Repeat this process for all the beads in the row (h).

In the same way add beading along the remaining horizontal dashed lines.

Thread your machine with the coral thread and couch a strand of coral cording between the vertical rows of decorative stitching.

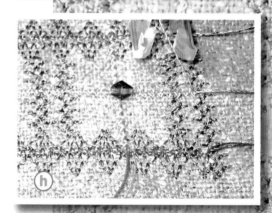

String 5 half-inch beads onto an 18" length of coral cording and add beads to the horizontal intersections as shown (i).

Position a 7" strip of lace 1" above the beaded grid and sew in place with a blind hemstitch. Position two-hole beads along the lace to determine how many you want to use.

String the two-hole glass beads onto two 14" strands of coral rayon thread (j).

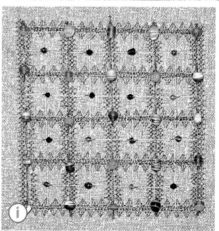

Thread your machine with a cotton variegated yellow/pink/purple thread and set to the widest zigzag stitch. Drop the feed dogs.

This is backwards stitching. Anchor the two bead strings. Bar-tack the ends, scoot the bead in *front* of the needle, hold the bead in place with the Beadle, and bar-tack again (k).

Sew the remaining 7" pieces of lace below the grid. On my bag I stitched the lace with a small buttonhole stitch and left the lower edge loose. Bead in the same way as the first lace strip.

Draw a rectangle about an inch beyond the lace and grid with a water-soluble pen.

Thread your machine with lilac embroidery thread and sew a row of decorative stitching on both sides of the line.

Couch sage green rayon yarn between the two rows of stitching with a wide zigzag stitch. Couch the yarn for an inch, raise the needle and presser foot, move the work forward for an inch, then couch for another inch (l).

Add bead drops at the ends of the lace strip (m).

A bead drop is an ornamental, secure group of beads. The beads hang free from the project. Think of it as an alternative to a tassel.

Thread a needle with a 12" double length of strong bead thread.

Lay out the beads in the sequence you want for the drop. Begin and end with a small bead.

String the beads, starting with the bead you want at the top, then bring the needle back through the beads, catching the small end bead to anchor the string. Tie the ends of the string together and attach to the project with secure hand stitches.

Making the Handle

Fold in and press ½" along the edges of the 2" x 18" strip of linen.

Press an 18" piece of Steam-a-Seam ½" fusible tape to cover the raw edges. Remove the paper and fuse the 18" piece of lace in place.

Couch the green yarn along the edges of the lace with a blanket stitch.

String 15" of E-beads on a 30" length of neutral Dual Duty Plus® thread and stitch the bead string along the center of the lace using the Raindrops technique (n).

Finishing the Bag

Sew the front and back of the bag together at the sides and bottom, right sides together. Turn right-side out and press.

Fold about 1" to the inside along the top edge of the bag and press.

Fold the lining fabric in half and sew the sides, right sides together.

Slip the lining inside the bag, wrong sides together, and fold the top down to match the size of the bag. Pin the folded lining and bag edges together. Pin the handle to the sides between the lining and the outside of the bag (o).

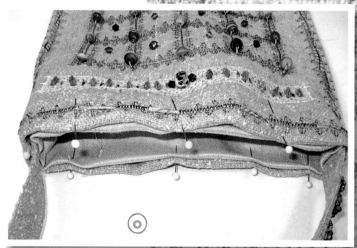

Stitch around the top edge of the bag with a large blanket stitch and natural-colored cotton thread, catching the lining and handle. Stitch around a second time if desired.

Grid pattern, *enlarge 200%*

AMBER AND AMETHYST DECORATIVE PILLOW, *14" x 14", made by the author*

# Amber & Amethyst Decorative Pillow

This panel is finished into a pretty boudoir pillow. It could also be used on the cover of a photo album or scrapbook. The colors of the fabric were matched to the beads. The border is made from a wonderful African fabric, which was the inspiration for the color scheme.

The trim is vintage crocheted lace, which I dyed yellow. The ribbons and big beads give it a sumptuous look.

Techniques

Bead by Machine **Technique #4— Couch Bead String and Pull** (page 32)

This project also uses the bar-tack and decorative and satin stitches.

Supplies

Fabric

- ⑥ 7 strips 1½" x 14" and 2 strips 2" x yellow cottons
- ⑥ 1 fat quarter border fabric cut into
    - ⑥ 2 strips 1½" x 14"
    - ⑥ 2 strips 1½" x 17"
- ⑥ ⅜ yard backing fabric cut into 2 rectangles 11" x 17"

Tools & Notions

- ⑥ 14" x 14" square fusible interfacing
- ⑥ 14" x 14" square nonwoven stabilizer
- ⑥ open-toed embroidery foot
- ⑥ cording foot
- ⑥ 16" x 16" pillow form

Thread (a)

- ⑥ 30-weight yellow variegated machine embroidery rayon
- ⑥ 30-weight lavender/yellow variegated machine rayon
- ⑥ decorative cording in lavender and yellow—Dazzle by Wonderfil, 8-weight crochet cotton, or embroidery floss can be substituted.
- ⑥ yellow cotton-covered polyester thread for the bead strings
- ⑥ lavender cotton-covered polyester thread for the bead strings

Beads

Beads for the yellow bead sets:

- twisted bugle beads (b)

- amber chips (c)

- half-inch yellow glass (d)

- gold seed beads (e)

Beads for the lavender bead sets:

- half-inch lavender glass (f)

- square yellow delica beads (g)

- amethyst chips (h)

- glass seed beads in mixed colors

Trim

- 4½ yards ⅝" wide sheer organdy ribbon with gold trim
- 2½ yards of 2" wide scalloped yellow crocheted trim

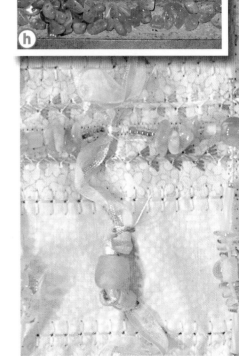

Making the Panel

Position the yellow strips of fabric side by side onto the square of fusible interfacing, sides touching, completely covering the interfacing. Follow the manufacturer's instructions and press with an iron to fuse.

Add stabilizer to the back.

Thread your machine with the variegated yellow machine embroidery thread and install an open-toed embroidery foot.

Join the yellow strips by sewing a line of a wide decorative stitch, centering the stitch where two strips meet (i).

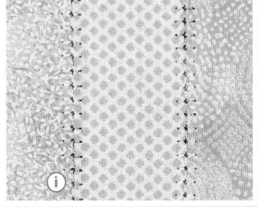

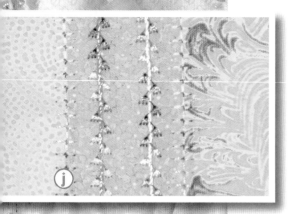

Couch two rows of cord down three of the five center yellow strips using a cording foot and a feather stitch. Use the edge of the foot as a guide for straight rows (j).

When using bugle beads it is important to note that the ends are rough cut. It is always a good idea to add a seed bead to each end and treat the three beads as one. This will prevent the bugle beads from cutting into the bead string.

String 4 yellow bead sets in a three-in-one bugle (using the gold seed beads), amber chips, yellow glass, amber chips, bugle three-in-one sequence on a 28" length of yellow thread. Measure the length of one set (k).

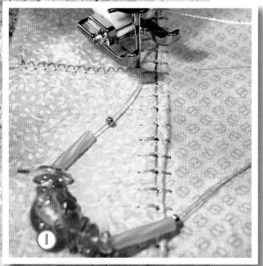

Anchor the bead string at the side edge of the panel. You want the bead sets to lie across the plain yellow strips.

Use a small zigzag stitch to couch the bead string, being careful not to catch the string with a stitch.

Slide a bead set up along the thread, loop to the side of the last stitch made, and continue stitching along the sewing line the length of the bead set. You may want to make a mark with a water-soluble marker to indicate the length (l).

Bring the bead string back to the drawn stitching line and zigzag stitch until you come to the next section where a bead set should be (m).

Slide the second bead set up along the thread, loop to the side of the last stitch made, and continue stitching along the drawn line as before. Bring the bead string back to the stitching line and continue stitching down the bead string beyond the second bead set.

Continue until the row is complete. Pull on the bead string to shorten it so the bead sets snap into place.

Secure the end of the bead string.

Apply 3 more rows of yellow bead sets

String 4 lavender bead sets as shown on a 28" length of lavender thread (n).

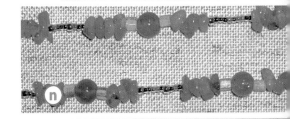

Use the same technique for sewing 3 rows of lavender bead sets, but with satin stitch couching between the sets. The lavender beads cross over the lines of stitching between the yellow bead sets (o).

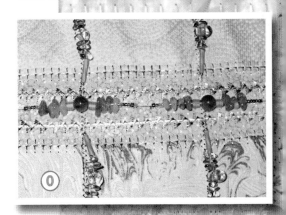

String ½" yellow glass beads onto the ribbon. Tie a loose knot on both side of each bead. Leave 3" between the beads (p).

Position the ribbon on the work and pin in place.

Bar-tack on either side of the knotted beads and at the mid-point of the ribbon (q).

Add 1½" border strips to the beaded panel.

Stitch crocheted or lace trim around the four sides of the work.

To make the back, fold under ½" twice on a long side of each 11" x17" rectangle and press. Sew with a decorative stitch.

Overlap the two finished edges and pin so that the back measures 17" square. Baste the overlap. Pin the back to the front, right sides together, tucking in the lace trim, and stitch with a ¼" seam allowance. Stitch again for a sturdier seam.

Remove basting, turn right side out, and insert the pillow form.

Grid pattern, *enlarge 200%*

patchwork strips

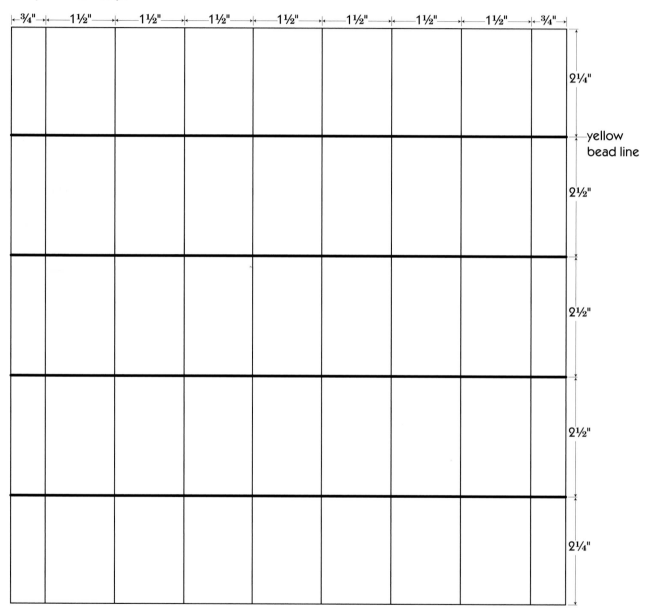

yellow
bead line

ALL BEADED **UP BY MACHINE** ○ **TERRY WHITE**

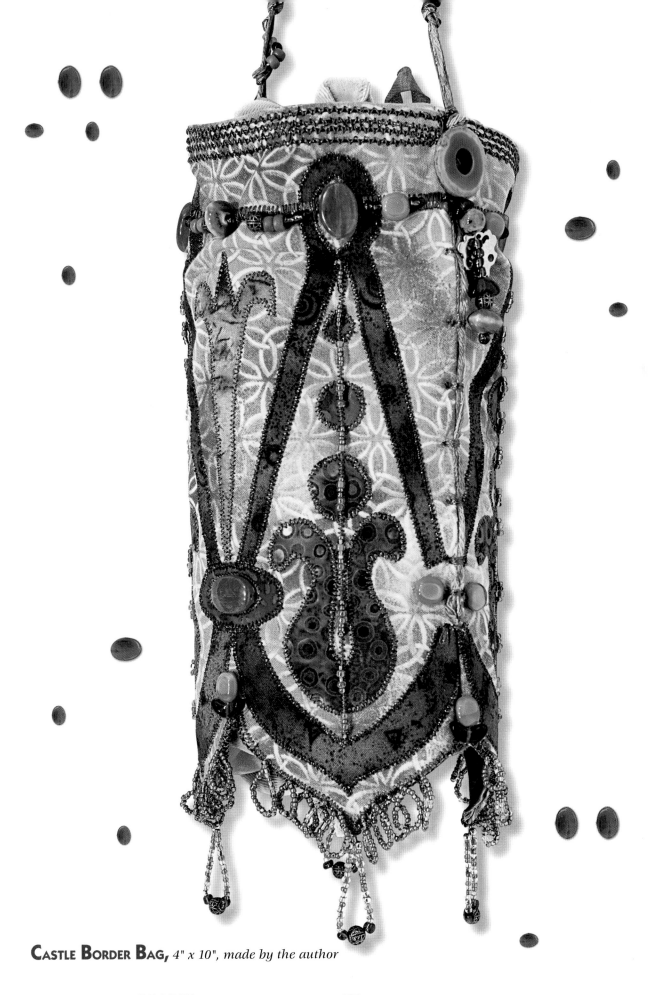

CASTLE BORDER BAG, *4" x 10", made by the author*

Castle Border Bag

This appliquéd and beaded bag has beaded fringe on the bottom and a knotted handle. Bead drops and a dusty pink silk velvet lining add luxury to the bag.

Techniques

Bead by Machine **Technique #1— Raindrops** (page 29)

Bead by Machine **Technique #3— Bar-Tack Yarn, and Bead Wrap** (page 31)

Bead by Machine **Technique #4— Couch Bead String and Pull** (page 32)

Bead by Machine **Technique #5— Loop Fringe** (page 34)

Supplies

Fabric

- 5" x20" salmon print cotton background
- ⅓ yard deep rust
- ¼ yard dark green
- ¼ yard turquoise
- scraps of rust and green print
- 13" x 13" square of dusty pink velvet for inner bag
- ½ yard gold charmeuse satin for lining

Tools & Notions

- 11" x 18" lightweight nonwoven interfacing for stabilizer
- 4" x 8" lightweight plastic or template plastic
- 4" x 4" square of fleece
- 1 yard fusible web
- fabric glue
- cording foot
- open-toed embroidery foot
- The Beadle

Thread

- sewing thread in colors to match fabric
- machine embroidery thread:
    - copper metallic
    - dark green rayon
    - burgundy rayon
    - rosy tan rayon
    - dark green rayon

Decorative Yarns

- Dazzle in wine by Wonderfil—It is rayon with a metallic fleck, similar to 8-weight crochet cotton.
- dusty rose worsted-weight crochet cotton
- 7 strands 30" long in a variety of blends and weights and a mixed blend of colors—rose, pink, wine, and salmon
- 6 strands of dusty pink, pink metallic, and pink rayon 12" long for the sides of the bag

supplies continued

ALL BEADED UP BY MACHINE ○ TERRY WHITE

Beads

- approximately 10 grams (⅓ ounce) each of E-beads in pink, copper, and matte yellow for handle (a)
- approximately 20 grams (¾ ounce) seed beads size 10 and larger pink/green/gold mix for decorative line on bag and fringe (b)
- novelty buttons and beads of ceramic, glass, plastic and metal (c)
- approximately 20 grams (¾ ounce) red and green seed bead mix

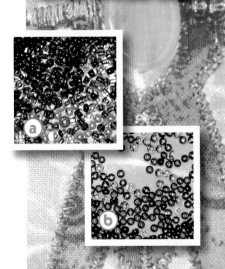

Making the Bag

This evening bag is constructed in two parts—an inner bag and an outer decorative panel. The decorative panel is attached to the bag to finish the project. Make the panel first.

Decorative Panel

Cut background fabric and 2 pieces of interfacing 11" x 18".

Trace the appliqué designs onto fusible web and place onto the back of the rust and turquoise fabrics. Fuse according to the manufacturer's directions and cut out shapes. The design area should measure approximately 8½" x 15" with 4 repeats of the design as shown in the placement diagram (page 83).

Position the stabilizer under the background and use a narrow zigzag stitch around the appliqué shapes. Two threads through the machine needle will create a rich effect. Use dark green rayon and copper metallic thread for the green fabrics and the same copper with burgundy rayon for the wine-colored fabrics.

Stitch seed beads down the center of the appliqué using the raindrops technique.

In the 2 spaces between the large motifs, draw a vertical line with a water-soluble marker and couch decorative yarns down the line with a bar-tack (d).

Decorative Band for Top of Bag

Using the novelty beads (c, page 79), lay the beads out over the appliqué design to fit. Use the wine cording for your bead string and technique #4 – Couch Bead String and Pull, page 32—to stitch this decorative band. After this decorative line of stitching is done, hand stitch the oval discs and the bead drops (e).

Beaded Fringe

Draw a line ⅝" from the bottom of the appliqué shapes to indicate where the fringe will go. Use a cording foot and 2 threads (copper and wine) through the eye of the needle to couch 2 strands of wine cording along the drawn line (f).

This fringe is stitched in 4 sections. The long fringe loop as well as the smaller bead loops are on one bead string.

Make 4 bead strings as follows: 7½" of the red/green bead mix; gold bead; 1½" inch of pink mix; copper glass; copper bead; copper glass; 1½" of pink mix; gold bead; 7½" of green/red mix (g).

Change to an open-toed embroidery foot.

Start in the center and stitch the center loop first. Use a wide satin stitch at the point (h).

Switch to a small zigzag stitch to stitch each loop (about 1½" inch of beads), spaced about ½" apart, 6 on each side of the center loop. Stitch on the inside edge of the couched cording.

Repeat for the remaining sections of bead fringe.

Cut ½" from the couched cording. Clip the seam close to the cord (i). Turn under and glue with fabric glue to the back of the panel (j).

Lining

Use the decorative panel as your pattern and cut the lining the same size and shape, adding ½" all the way around. Glue under ½" and glue the lining to the decorative panel.

Stitch the sides of the panel closed. Fold down ⅝" along the top of the purse to the inside over the lining. Use some fabric glue to baste. On the outside of the purse couch down cording with 4 rows of zigzag or a decorative stitch. This decorates, stitches the hem, and stabilizes the top of the purse all at the same time (k).

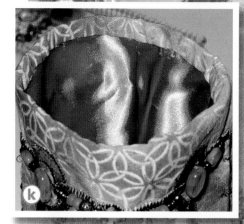

Beaded Handle

Cut 7 lengths of decorative cording 30" long.

String beads on one strand. Use glue on the end of the strand to create a "needle." The glue will harden and the beads will string easily on the cord.

Arrange the beads in alternating groups of brown and pink beads, 1" of beads per group. Tie a bead to each end of the cord to keep them from falling off.

Take all the cords in hand and knot every 1½". Between each knot, pull a group of the beads up and then make the next knot. Every knot has a group of beads between them except for the ends. Leave about 2" free at each end (l).

Inner Bag

Stitch together the 13" square of velvet and a 13" x 13" square of lining, right sides together, leaving a 4" opening on one side. Turn and stitch the opening closed. With a needle and strong thread, gather up the bottom of the purse with a running stitch. Take several stitches in place to secure. This makes a little rosette on the bottom of the bag (m).

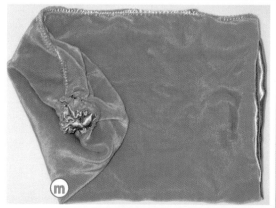

Cut 2 circles 3½" in diameter from lightweight plastic. Cut one circle of fleece and glue to one of the circles. Cut 2 circles of the lining fabric 1" larger than the diameter of the plastic circles. Gather a circle of lining fabric over each one with a running stitch (n).

Secure the thread. Glue the wrong sides of the circles together. Place this circle in the bottom of the purse to stabilize the cylinder.

Slip the purse inside the outer panel and tack in place.

For the purse closure, add some vintage or decorative buttons and wrap with a tie of decorative cording (o).

Appliqué pattern

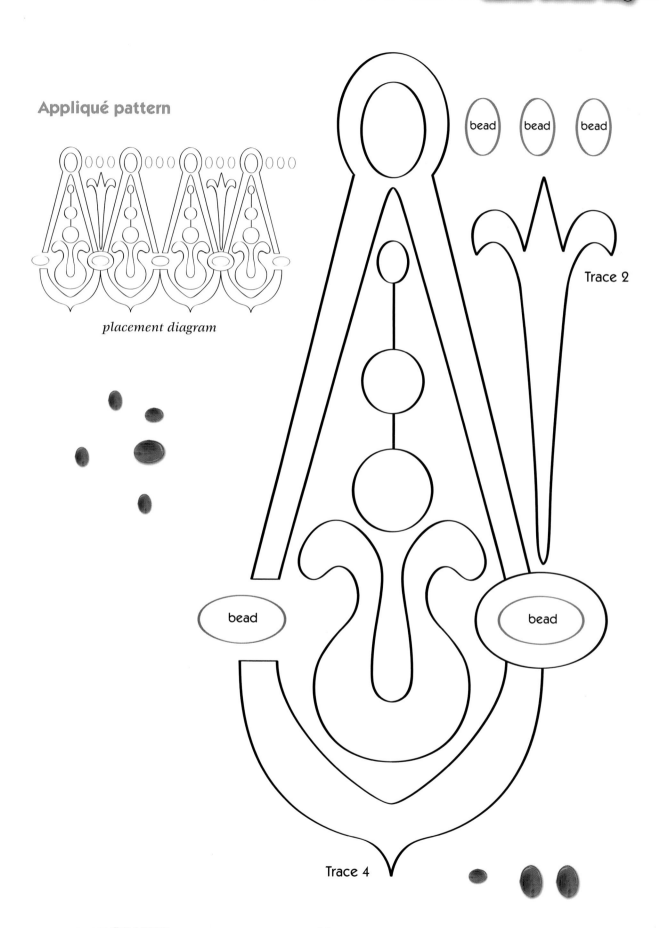

placement diagram

bead   bead   bead

Trace 2

bead

bead

Trace 4

BUBBLE MAT, *8" x 10", made by the author*

ubble Mat

Nothing is cuter than a baby taking a bath in the kitchen sink. This is a picture of my grandson, AJ, when he was just a year old. I masked the background of the photo with hand-drawn bubbles on white card stock before inserting his picture into the mat.

Techniques

Bead by Machine **Technique #6 — Free Motion Beading** (page 35)

Free-motion embroidery

Supplies

Fabric

- 12" x 15" 100 percent cotton with a bit of texture

Tools & Notions

- free-motion or darning foot
- fine point permanent fabric markers in several shades of blue
- 12" x 15" medium nonwoven interfacing
- embroidery hoop
- The Beadle
- fabric glue

Threads

- rayon machine embroidery threads in shades of blue and variegated shades of blue
- medium-blue variegated cotton thread

Beads

- transparent seed beads in a mix of blue, pink, and white
- a darker mix of darker shades of blues
- seed pearls
- drop beads
- large light-colored bubble beads (these will be hand stitched)
- ¼" dark turquoise glass discs (these will be hand stitched)

Machine Setup

- drop the feed dogs
- loosen top tension
- set for straight stitch
- install a darning or free-motion foot
- install a #14 embroidery needle
- thread with medium-blue variegated thread

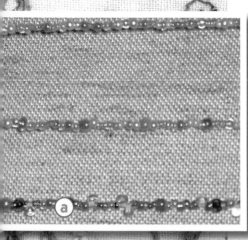

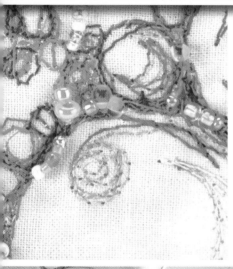

Beading Setup

When stringing the beads for free-motion work, the beads should only fill ¼ the length of the string. More thread is needed because a lot more is stitched down between the beads than in the other techniques.

Separating the beads into strings of different values, rather than mixing values, helps to add some interesting color lines (a).

Making the Mat

Trace the design onto the cotton with shades of blue permanent marking pens. It's all right if the stitching doesn't completely cover the lines because the drawing can be part of the design.

Free-motion embroider the large and medium bubbles with a medium-blue variegated thread. The small bubbles will be thread painted as the beads are attached with free-motion beading.

The following description is a simple overview of free-motion embroidery. (See my book *Thread Painting Made Easy*, also published by AQS, for detailed information.)

Hoop the fabric with a stabilizer and position under the needle. Lower the needle into the fabric and bring it up once. Tug on the top thread to bring the bobbin thread to the top. Hold the top and bobbin threads together and stitch several small stitches. Cut the tails of the threads.

Start stitching over the drawn lines and move the hoop slowly at first. A rhythm is achieved by stitching at a medium speed and moving the hoop. This technique requires some practice. You want to stitch fast enough so the stitches aren't pulling and you don't feel the needle pulling on the fabric.

Stitch the photo opening and the large bubbles with the medium-blue variegated thread.

Stitch over the photo opening and the large bubbles and bubble detail a second time with a rayon variegated blue thread (b).

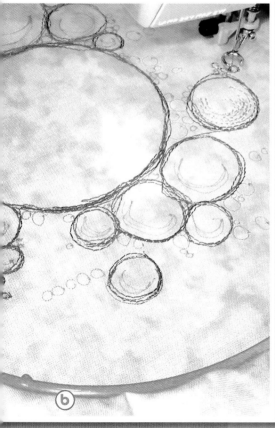

Thread your machine with thread to match the color of the beads.

Secure the bead string along the edge of a bubble. Stitch away from the start of the bead string for about ½", not catching the bead string (c).

Pull the bead string back into the line of stitching. Use the Beadle to hold the beads in front of the sewing machine needle so that they don't pop back and interfere with the needle. You will be stitching away from the beads (d).

Stitch over the bead string for another ½". Continue around the bubbles in this manner (e).

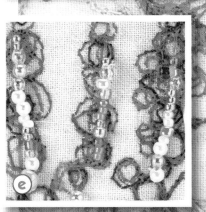

If your darning foot is too cumbersome, try stitching with the ankle on your machine or with just the needle and nothing on the shaft. (This is done in ribbon embroidery all the time.) The hoop will keep the work from distorting too much.

When the stitching is complete, remove from the hoop and press, face down, on a folded towel. Cut a hole in the center of the big bubble, leaving a generous ¼" seam allowance (f).

Snip the seam allowance about every ¼" around, turn under, and glue in place.

To finish the mat, cut to fit the inside of a deep frame and position the photo behind the opening.

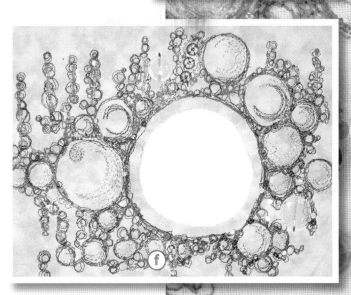

Embroidery Pattern

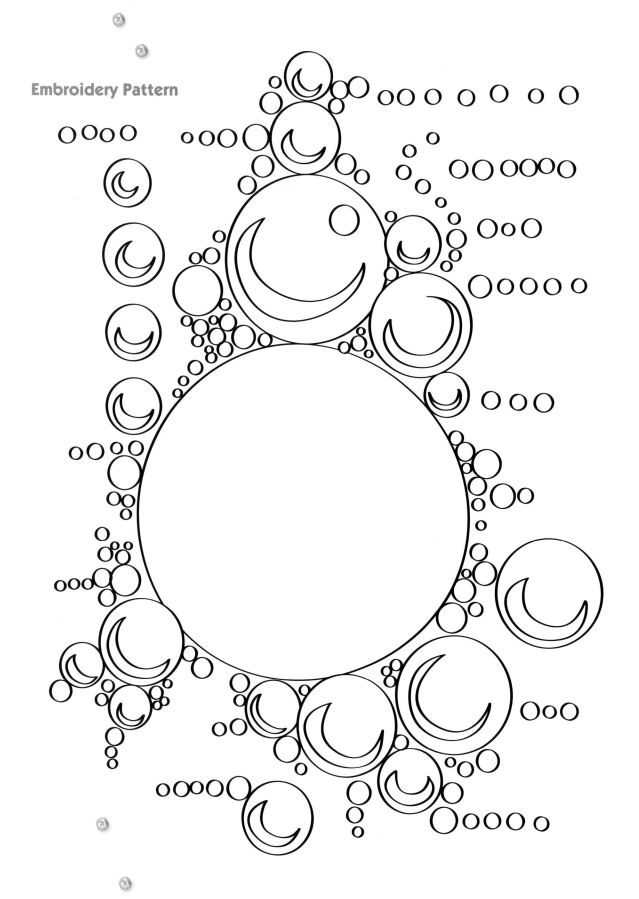

ALL BEADED UP BY MACHINE ○ TERRY WHITE

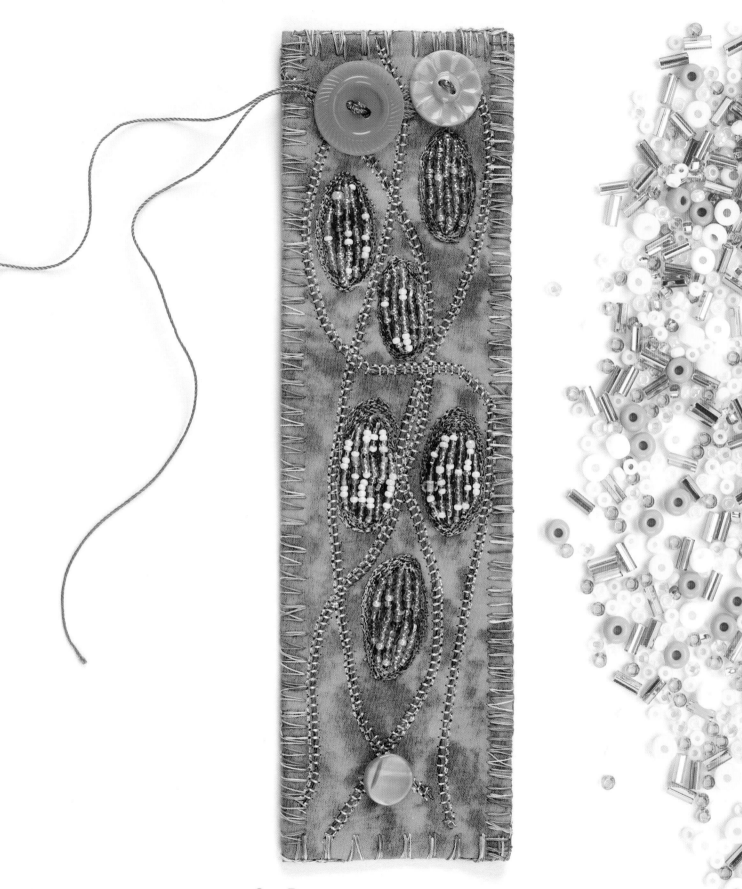

CUFF BRACELET, *2¼" x 8", made by the author*

Cuff Bracelet

This one-of-a-kind bracelet is the perfect small project to show off your beadwork.

Techniques

Bead by Machine **Technique #7— Seed Bead Fill** (page 37)

Supplies

Fabric

- 12" x 12" spring green 100 percent cotton

Tools & Notions

- 12" x 12" nonwoven medium-weight interfacing
- fabric glue
- cording foot

Thread

- machine embroidery threads:
  - pink/orange/yellow/lavender cotton variegated
  - green rayon variegated
  - gold metallic
  - coral rayon

Yarn

- size 12 pearl cotton or rayon cord in coral or dark pink

Beads

- a mix of size 10 seed beads in yellow, pink, green, lavender, blue, orange, and pearl
- 3 decorative buttons for fastening

Machine Setup for Beading

- remove the foot; use ankle only

Making the Bracelet

Transfer the design to the fabric with a permanent fabric marker using a light box; or tape the design to a sunny window, tape the fabric over it, and trace. Put the stabilizer under the fabric before stitching.

Couch cords over the drawn lines with a buttonhole or other decorative stitch. Use a cording foot that will hold the cord under the center needle position. Threads used are shown in the photo (a).

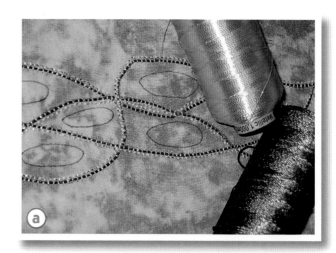

Place the work in an embroidery hoop. Hoop the fabric with the large ring on the bottom and the small ring on the top. This holds the fabric taut and close to the surface of the machine table (b). Using an extension table supports the hoop while working.

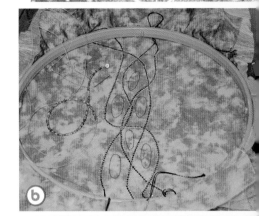

String 10" of seed beads onto a 20" length of thread. Thread the machine with variegated green rayon. Anchor the bead string at the end of an oval.

Bring the bobbin thread to the top, hold the top and bobbin threads together, and take a few stitches. Cut the tails. Stitch to the oval where the bead string is anchored (c).

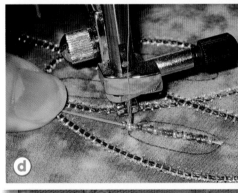

Fill the ovals from the center out. Stitch a center line first. Pull the bead string to the needle and scoot the beads along the string to fill the line (d).

Loop the beads out of the way and free-motion couch over the bead string at the tip of the oval, being careful not to catch the string with the stitching (e).

Pull the bead string taut so the beads pop into place (f).

Stitch along the side of the first row of beads (g).

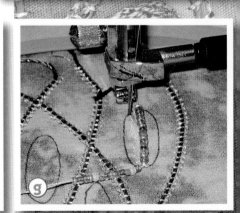

Scoot enough beads along the bead string to fill the space, loop the beads out of the way, and free-motion couch over the bead string. Pull the string taut. Continue in this manner, filling in one side of the oval, then fill the other half. When the fill is complete, thread paint along the edge of the oval to cover any rough looking ends (h).

Trim the beaded fabric to 7" x 9". Fold in the edges as shown and press (i).

Apply fabric glue to the edges. Fold in half, aligning the edges, and let the glue dry.

Stitch a large blanket stitch around the edges with variegated cotton thread.

Position the buttons and hand stitch them in place with coral pearl cotton or rayon cord, leaving long tails on one button. Fasten the bracelet by wrapping the tails around the buttons (j).

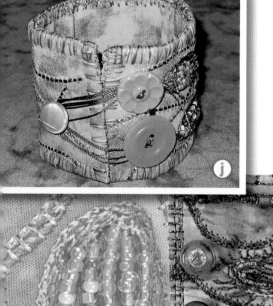

This bracelet was made with a similar design. The fill area was defined with free-motion stitching prior to beading (k).

The wider fabric allowed for an additional row of beads on either side of the fill area. Extra embellishments including a small turtle charm add to its appeal.

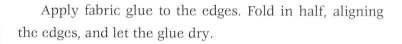

Cuff Bracelet Pattern

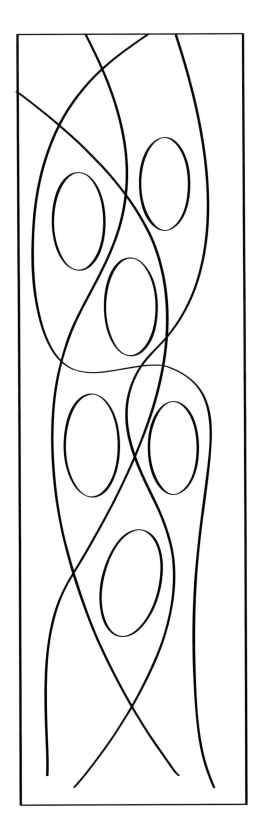

Resources

Terry's Web site

www.threadpaint.com

Source for inspiration, patterns, videos, notions, books and class information

The Bead Spinner

Pacbell

www.beadspinner.net

The seed bead stringing tool has wonderful directions on the site with a video on how to use it.

Bernina

www.berninausa.com

What a great sewing machine!

Coats & Clarks Thread Company

www.coatandclark.com

Great threads, yarns, novelty fibers, embroidery floss

Creative Feet

PO Box 26282

Prescott Valley, AZ

86312-6282

Toll Free Phone: 800-776-6938

www.creativefeet.com

Specialty feet for all zigzag machines

Fire Mountain Gems

www.firemountaingems.com

A wonderful resource for all things beady—beads, beading supplies, and the Speedy Stringer™ bead spinner

Morgan Hoops and Stands, Inc.

8040 Erie Ave. – Chanhassen, MN

55317-9632

Phone: (612) 387-2183

Fax: (866) 571-8531

www.nosliphoops.com

Source for embroidery hoops

Rust-Tex

Lois Jarvis

www.rust-tex.com

Source for learning how to dye with naturally occurring iron oxide for obtaining beautifully altered textiles

The Village Mercantile

123 South 2nd Street

Boonville, IN 47601

Phone: 812-897-5687

www.villagemercantile.com

My really great local quilt shop. Support your local quilt shop!

YLI Corporation

www.ylicorp.com

Great specialty threads!

American Quilter's Society

www.AmericanQuilter.com

Source for the companion video to All Beaded Up by Machine *and* The Beadle

About the Author

Terry White started stitching as a little girl. Beads were an integral part of her hand needlework. Beads and buttons found their way into her embroidery, needlepoint, tatting, and quilting. When she turned to the sewing machine for creative stitchery following a hand injury, among the several techniques she developed was beading by machine. Designing the little "Beadle" tool was part of this process.

Over the years she has discovered more and better techniques for beadwork using the wonderful array of beads, threads, and fibers available today. Terry doesn't say," Practice makes perfect," she says, "Practice makes better and the more you do, the more you can do." Terry especially enjoys teaching others how to enhance their work with beads.

When she's not traveling to teach, Terry lives in Rockport, Indiana, with her husband, Scott, who produces her how-to video CDs.